POWER TAROT

POWER TAROT

POWER TAROT

More Than 100 Spreads That Give

Specific Answers to Your Most

Important Questions

Trish MacGregor
and Phyllis Vega

ATRIA PAPERBACK

New York   London   Toronto   Sydney   New Delhi

ATRIA
PAPERBACK

An Imprint of Simon & Schuster, Inc.
1230 Avenue of the Americas
New York, NY 10020

This Atria Paperback edition February 2021
Previously published in 1998 by Fireside, an imprint of Simon & Schuster, Inc.

ATRIA PAPERBACK and colophon are trademarks of Simon & Schuster, Inc.

For information about special discounts for bulk purchases, please contact Simon & Schuster Special Sales at 1-866-506-1949 or business@simonandschuster.com.

The Simon & Schuster Speakers Bureau can bring authors to your live event. For more information or to book an event, contact the Simon & Schuster Speakers Bureau at 1-866-248-3049 or visit our website at www.simonspeakers.com.

Interior design by Irving Perkins Associates

Manufactured in the United States of America

29   30   28

The Library of Congress has cataloged the Fireside edition as follows:

MacGregor, T. J.
Power tarot: more than 100 spreads that give specific answers to your most important questions / Trish MacGregor and Phyllis Vega.
p. cm.
"A Fireside book."
Includes index.
I. Tarot. I. Vega, Phyllis. II. Title.
BF1879.T2M3 1998
133.3'2424—dc21   97-46843
CIP

ISBN 978-0-684-84185-4
ISBN 978-1-4767-5306-5 (ebook)

The fall of the tarot cards,
even if random by usual definitions,
may be part of a chaotic system and
therefore may have a hidden order.

> — CYNTHIA GILES,
> **The Tarot**

. . . magic consists of removing the
limitations from what we think are the
earthly and spiritual laws that bind or
compel us. We can be anything because
we are ALL.

> — MARY K. GREER,
> **Women of the Golden Dawn**

Thanks to:

Our agent, Al Zuckerman, and our editor, Sydny Miner, for believing in the book; and Rob MacGregor, Linda Griffin, Edith Mercier, Renie Wiley, Charles Vega, Debbie Vega, Sharon Garcia, Jorge Garcia, and Rose Marie and Tony Janeshutz, for their infinite patience.

To our little tarot readers:

—

Alexis Garcia,
Yesenia Garcia,
Megan MacGregor.

CONTENTS

—

LIST OF SPREADS

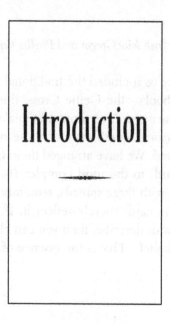

Introduction

Spreads form the heart of tarot. They create the stories the cards tell and depict recurring patterns that are both visible and invisible, known and unknown, obvious and hidden.

Some spreads work best for specific questions, others describe general situations and conditions, and still others answer questions that haven't been asked yet. The collection of spreads given in this book covers a spectrum broad enough to fit most people's needs.

We've designed these spreads to obtain concrete, direct answers to the questions most people ask about their daily lives: romance, work, finances, health, and spirituality. You won't have to wade through pages of mythological associations, historical data about the tarot, or esoteric information. Just get out your deck, find a spread that seems to fit your question, and lay out the cards.

Although we've included the traditional spreads you find in most tarot books—the Celtic Cross, the Horoscope, the Magic Star—the majority are nontraditional spreads that grew out of our personal questions and those of the people for whom we've read. We have arranged them from the simplest spread (one card) to the most complex (twenty-four cards).

As you work with these spreads, remember that *you* create your reality, the cards merely reflect it. If you don't like a situation the cards describe, then *you* can change it by working with your beliefs. That is the essence of Power Tarot.

1

What Is Tarot?

The tarot has entered an unprecedented boom period, with more than three hundred decks now on the market. Their motifs range from angels to legends, the Middle Ages to the millennium.

The lure of a particular deck lies as much in the artwork as it does in how the deck feels when you handle it. Favorite decks usually speak to something private and sacred within you; they are like old friends you haven't visited for a long time. They *feel* right.

If you're just beginning your work with the tarot, the best deck you can use is either the Rider-Waite or any Waite-Smith clone. The latter includes: Universal Waite, Albano Waite, Golden Rider, Morgan Greer, Hanson Roberts, Tarot of the Cloisters, Robin Wood, and The Aquarian Tarot.

Learn the textbook definitions of the seventy-eight cards, practice the traditional spreads, read for yourself, your family, your friends, whoever will sit still long enough. Practice until the definitions become as familiar to you as your name. And then read for strangers.

The first time you read for someone you don't know, all kinds of emotions will wash through you: exhilaration, nervousness, triumph, uncertainty. You'll quickly discover which cards demand more of your attention, which ones you know by heart, which ones pertain most strongly to a particular individual. Whether you stumble through the reading or glide through it smoothly, you'll have a much clearer sense of the tarot's voice—and the voice of the deck you're using.

As you work with the tarot, you'll find that some cards recur; no matter how you shuffle the deck or what spread you use, the same cards keep coming up. These usually depict patterns in your life or in the life of the person for whom you're reading. They assume a personal meaning that may not be in line with the textbook definition. If you're relentless, you'll eventually have highly personal definitions for all of the seventy-eight cards. And that's what the tarot is really about: *What does this card mean to me?*

There are certain cards you will love and welcome; there are others you will detest and dread. The Tower stands out as an excellent example.

Its image from deck to deck doesn't vary much. The Tower stands tall against a darkened, ugly sky that looms with menace. Lightning strikes its ancient walls, objects or people or both tumble from its windows, the water below it seems to bubble and writhe like a primal sea. Things are not in good shape.

In the beginning, this card will send chills up your spine, you'll be expecting the absolute worst: a pink slip in the mail, a legal judgment that isn't in your favor, car problems, electrical problems, problems, problems, problems.

But as you work with the Tower, you'll realize that it's also about breaking old routines and patterns that limit who and what you are. The card is the equivalent of the planet Uranus in astrology in that it symbolizes the breaking apart of structures that tend to restrict you. The Tower puts you on notice that change is required. If you don't change voluntarily, then change will be imposed on you by some external force.

As with any language, your grasp of the tarot will change, evolve, and deepen the more you use it.

The Arcanas

The typical Tarot deck has seventy-eight cards that are divided into the major arcana (22) and the minor arcana (56). Think of the majors as archetypal events, *big* issues that concern character and destiny. Minors are concerned with circumstances and behavior and illustrate how the energy of the majors manifests in your daily life.

The majors, numbered from zero to twenty-one, are ports in a journey that begins with the wildly innocent enthusiasm of the Fool and ends with the sophistication and knowledge of the World. They are the most powerful cards in the deck. Sometimes, the majors tell you all you need to know to understand the dynamics in a person's life.

The minors are divided into four suits: wands, cups, swords, and pentacles. They correspond to the four elements, the four personality types, the four seasons. The suits are the DNA of the minor arcana, the building blocks.

Each suit is numbered from one through ten and has four court cards. The pips, or numbered cards, represent the patterns which the archetypes weave in our lives; the court cards usually represent people or behavior patterns. In some decks, you'll find the court cards called something else—the page and knight, for instance, are a prince and princess. But if you're just beginning with the tarot, it's easiest to work with decks that have traditional names for the court cards.

The mundane and esoteric meanings for the cards will vary, depending on which decks you use and which books you read. Once you become familiar with the cards, you'll supplement and expand the meanings from your own experience. Our meanings began with the traditional definitions, then grew and expanded through trial and error. So will yours.

The Tarot Journal

In the beginning, a journal can be an invaluable aid. It doesn't have to be anything complicated; a notebook or a file in your computer will do. Since you'll be reading mostly for yourself at first, jot down the date, your question, the cards you pulled, and your interpretation. Check back periodically to see how accurate the reading was.

There's nothing like success to bolster confidence. You may be surprised to discover how often you're right on target. The best readings are those in which your intuition speaks through the cards.

Sometimes, a journal points out a flawed interpretation of just one or two cards in a given reading. In the summer of 1994, for example, a friend of ours, Eva, was in the process of separating from her husband. She asked us to do a reading on how the divorce would go.

We did the five-card Direction Spread for her (included in the section of five-card spreads) and in the fourth position—

who or what will help—drew the king of swords. Eva had recently spoken to a male attorney about possible representation and we interpreted the king to be the attorney.

But several months down the road, it was obvious that the king was Eva's husband. They had managed to work out mutually acceptable terms for the divorce and never needed an attorney. Her husband, in fact, didn't want an attorney involved any more than she did and ended up buying a townhouse for her and their daughter. Eva now pays her mortgage directly to him.

Given the information we had to work with, our interpretation wasn't wrong. The king of swords is typically a male over forty who communicates without emotion. He might be a businessman, a surgeon, a lawyer. He cuts to the heart of the matter. Eva's husband is a successful businessman in his sixties who communicated in a straightforward manner about what he could live with in a divorce agreement. It simply seemed inconceivable to her at the time that her husband would be of any help at all.

After a certain point, the journal may become cumbersome or your entries too erratic to be of much help. So set the journal aside. There aren't any rules. You don't have to keep a journal to read tarot cards. It's simply a tool and once you outgrow your use for it, don't keep doing it because you feel you have to. Above all, tarot should be fun, thrilling, liberating, empowering.

Spreads

The spreads in this book can be used by beginners, pros, and everyone in between. If you're just starting out, the shorter spreads are easiest. In fact, the best way to learn the definitions of the cards is to pull a card a day, jot the card and definition in your journal, and at the end of the day note how this energy manifested.

If you've reached the point where you're reading for family and friends, you'll want to practice with more complex spreads. We recommend the spreads with five to seven cards, which can be adapted for just about any question.

The Ladle Spread, for instance, packs a lot of information into just six cards. It provides an overview of the question, pinpoints what is hidden, what is emerging, what is visible, what you "scoop out," or obtain; and explains the key element in the issue. You can lay out another six cards for additional information, for a total of twelve cards.

One of our clients wanted to know how his relationship with his current girlfriend was going to work out. The Ladle Spread told a rather accurate story.

The Lovers in the overview position made it clear he was going to have to make a choice about this relationship. The eight of cups appeared in the hidden position—that he would soon walk away from the relationship because for him, it was finished. The six of swords in the third position indicated that, mentally, he had already moved away from this relationship toward something else that was unknown, but less tumultuous.

In the fourth position, what is visible, he drew the ace of swords. This indicated that he had already met someone else who interested him. Sure enough, the queen of cups, an older nurturing woman, turned up in the fifth position. The last card was the ace of wands, indicating that he would shortly begin a new job.

He wanted additional information about the queen of cups, so he drew three more cards for the fifth position: the four of swords, the five of swords, and the three of wands. This suggested that the new woman was currently in a respite period, perhaps recuperating from surgery or illness, or simply reevaluating what she wanted out of her life. The five of swords made it likely that she had recently won some dispute and, because of it, would soon be working in partnership with other people (three of wands).

The young man said it was all true. The relationship with this new woman had already begun, he had applied for a new job, and now he was prepared to walk away from his old girlfriend. This was a reading in which it wasn't necessary to draw supplementary cards for all six positions; the queen of cups was the woman about whom he wanted more information.

Most questions seem to fall into several broad categories: romance, work/career, finances, health, and spiritual matters. The spreads in this book address specifics within each of these categories.

A question about love, for instance, might be answered more thoroughly by the ten-card Ongoing Relationship Spread than by the traditional Celtic Cross. If you're inquiring about your spiritual progress, the five-card Belief Spread is a good place to start.

When Is It Going to Happen?

The trickiest part of tarot has to do with timing. Unlike astrology and numerology, the tarot doesn't lend itself to exact timing. This is actually one of the reasons we prefer tarot to other disciplines. We believe that the point of power is in the present and that the future is plastic and open-ended and can be changed in any moment.

Having said this, one of the questions we hear most from

people is: When will a particular event happen? Everyone seems to want to know *when*. When will I meet the love of my life? When will that job promotion come through? When will I get out of debt, engaged, married, pregnant, divorced?

The best way to obtain a general time frame is to use one of the spreads that contains a built-in timing device. Some spreads that fall into this category are: six-card Timing, seven-card Pyramid, and seven-card Weekly. Before you begin the reading, state the time frame: X number of days, weeks, or months.

Other spreads have a timing factor built into them through a near-future position in the layout. In the Celtic Cross, this is the sixth position; you can decide before the reading what period of time it covers.

One quick method of answering the timing question is to pull cards until you reach an ace. Before you pull the cards, decide whether they represent days, weeks, months, or years. Then count the number of cards you turned over before you got to the ace.

The classic, but more cumbersome method, is to key the cards to the seasons of the year. This can be done in several ways. Our favorite is to remove the major arcana from the deck and to work with the court and pip cards. Pick one card from this deck of fifty-six. This becomes your timing card.

The key to this system is: wands = spring; cups = summer; pentacles = autumn; swords = winter. An ace then represents the first week of the season, a two is the second week of the season, and so on, through the queen as the thirteenth week of the season. Kings represent the transition from one season to the next.

Another timing method is to use the numbers on the cards as a timing device. With the major arcana, remove The Fool from the deck. The probable timing will run from one to twenty-two days, weeks, or months. With the pip cards you can go up to ten months; by adding the court cards, the time is extended to fourteen months. The meanings of the cards don't come into play; only the numbers are important.

Future changes depend on the questioner's beliefs, thoughts, feelings, choices, and decisions. When pressed for an exact date we'll provide answers using one or more of the methods discussed in this section. But any timing prediction should be prefaced with an explanation that a time frame can be changed through intent and desire.

What If a Reading Doesn't Make Sense?

It happens. The cards are in front of you, you know what they mean, but when you try to put them together they don't make sense. The best thing you can do it simply pick up the cards and try another spread. If this doesn't work, then try a spread using just the major arcana.

If the cards still seem confused, tell the person you're reading for that the cards don't seem to want to address that particular question or issue at the moment and suggest that you move on to something else. It's a bad idea to tell the person you can't read for them right now; the individual might interpret it to mean you have foreseen his or her imminent demise.

Should I Read Reversed Cards?

Reversed cards refer to cards that are upside down. Some readers feel the tarot is incomplete unless you read reversed cards, but you'll find pros and cons on this point. Other readers think there are already enough negative cards to deal with, so why add seventy-eight more? Ultimately, you'll have to decide for yourself if you should read them reversed.

At first, though, for the sake of simplicity, it's probably a good idea to stick to the upright meanings for the deck. After all, it's much easier to learn seventy-eight definitions than a hundred and fifty-six definitions.

We tend to read reversed cards only if they fall out of the deck that way, which is why you won't find the meanings for reversed positions in this book. The only other instance in which we use reversed cards is to answer yes/no questions.

Quite often an individual will want a simple yay or nay about something. We then shuffle a deck so there are reversed cards and deal out five. If the majority are upright, the answer is yes; vice versa would mean a resounding no.

If you use one of the round decks—Motherpeace or Tarot of the Cloisters—reversed meanings become something of a moot issue. With round decks, there are no definite ups or downs to the cards.

Deck Care and Preparation Rituals

When you first get your tarot deck, you should shuffle and mix the cards until you feel they're ready to use. The idea is to infuse them with your particular energy to create a special link between you and the deck. Some readers suggest you sleep with the new deck under your pillow, but frankly, it isn't necessary unless you feel that it is.

The traditional method calls for wrapping your decks in cloth and keeping them in cloth bags or wooden boxes. Silk is the favored wrap, although any fabric that appeals to you can be used. Bags are usually velvet or satin, decorated with embroidery or hand painted. You can store your decks in wooden boxes, decorated tin containers, or the packages they came in.

But really, there aren't any rules. Do what feels right to you. One of us keeps to the ritual, the cards neatly stored in bags and boxes and stashed in an accessible place. The other has decks all over the house, most of them held together by just a rubber band.

If you're a collector of tarot cards, it's important to keep the original packaging because the value of any deck decreases when the box or booklet is missing.

Preparation rituals, like most things connected with tarot, are a personal matter. We do little more than clear our minds, take a deep breath, and focus on the question and whoever we're reading for. You may prefer to light a candle or a stick of incense, do a short meditation, or offer a prayer before you begin.

Clearing Your Tarot Deck

When you're doing one reading after another, the cards often seem to lose their zip, so it's a good idea to clear or cleanse the deck from time to time. The classic way to clear a deck is to put the cards in order. In new decks, the cards are in a particular sequence that begins with the majors in numerical order, followed by each suit arranged from ace to king. After restoring the cards to their original order, shuffle the deck thoroughly, as you would a brand-new deck.

We occasionally use quartz crystals to clear our decks. Place a crystal on top of the deck in between readings to absorb whatever vibrations may remain from the prior reading. Crystals used for this purpose should be cleansed periodically in a mixture of sea salt and warm water, then dried and placed outside or on a windowsill where they can he recharged by the sun's rays.

You may purify your decks and crystals by "smudging" them, Native American style, in the smoke of sage or cedar. If smudge sticks are not available, burn some dried herbs like rosemary or sage in a fireproof dish. Pass the deck of cards or the crystal through the smoke several times.

If you don't want to be bothered with any of this, just use a different deck.

How Does Tarot Compare to Other Divination Tools?

Recently, a person we read for remarked that he was happy with his reading and pleased that his life was on such a positive track, but was this stuff really *true*? Was it really going to *happen*?

Any divination tool—astrology, the *I Ching*, runes, medicine cards, sticks and bones—is best used with the understanding that nothing is inscribed in stone. Your free will endows you with the power to write the scripts that you live, to change what you don't like, and to create more of what you do like. You set the course of your life—not the tool, not the reader, not destiny.

When the cards are drawn or the runes are tossed, you have a picture of how your life exists *in that moment* and how it is most likely to evolve based on your present patterns of belief. When you change those beliefs, the pattern changes, and you end up with different cards, different runes, different hexagrams.

In this way, tarot and other divination systems are a way to track what is going on inside yourself or the person for whom you're reading. The beauty of the tarot, however, and its major difference from other divination systems, is that its language is visual. The artwork on a deck speaks directly to that part of us that lives and breathes in an archetypal world. Tarot is the internal made manifest.

2

How Tarot Works

Archetypes and Synchronicity

The twenty-two cards of the major arcana constitute a world as exotic and complex as any foreign culture you will ever encounter. And yet, once you understand that the majors depict archetypes that are common to each of us, they don't seem quite as strange.

Archetypes breathe within the collective unconscious of the human race. They are found in mythology, folklore, fairy tales, legends, hallucinations, fantasies, and dreams. They connect us despite vast differences in language, culture, religious and political beliefs.

An example of an archetype would be the wise old man or woman in a dream who offers advice or guidance. In tarot, the wise old man is the Hermit, who goes within for his answers, and his female equivalent is the High Priestess.

The Swiss psychologist Carl Jung believed that archetypes often manifest through startling coincidences, which he called synchronicities. In his brilliant preface to the Richard Wilhelm addition to the *I Ching*, Jung wrote, ". . . synchronicity takes the coincidence of events in space and time as meaning something more than mere chance, namely a peculiar interdependence of objective events among themselves as well as with the subjective (psychic) states of the observer or observers."

Jung was referring specifically to the fall of the yarrow sticks or coins in the *I Ching*. But the principle of synchronicity lies at the heart of any divination system. For when you toss the coins or lay out the cards, they form a pattern intrinsic to that moment. The pattern, as Jung points out, is meaningful only if you're able to read and verify the interpretation through your knowledge of the subjective and objective situations, as well as the unfolding of subsequent events.

An example of such a synchronicity happened when a neighbor asked us to pull some cards on whether she was pregnant. She felt that she might be, but thought it could be wishful thinking. We did several spreads, but none of the traditional pregnancy cards showed up (Empress, ace of cups, page of cups, ace of wands).

Her five-year-old son was in the room with us and asked if he could draw a card. We fanned the deck facedown on the table and he plucked out the Empress.

Sure enough, a week later the pregnancy was verified by the woman's doctor. This is synchronicity in action. *For that single moment* when her son picked his card, the Empress was the one in seventy-eight that could give her the definitive answer she asked for and her son chose it.

Most of us experience synchronicities, but tend to shrug them off as meaningless until we understand their importance in the overall scheme of things. But if, as physicist David Bohm suggests, all things are connected at the quantum level, then we'd better pay attention to these apparent coincidences. They alert us to certain patterns that are operating in our lives.

A striking example of synchronicity happened to a friend of ours who is a writer. She has an affinity for tree frogs, considers them lucky, and whenever one hops into her house she is sure she will hear good news shortly.

But one afternoon she found a small frog caught in the edge of a screen door. When she opened the door to free it, she saw that its rear leg was broken. She felt the key word was "broken," that she would shortly hear that some tie in her life had been broken. The next morning, her agent told her that her publisher had passed on a recent submission.

Coincidence?

There's no such word in tarot.

Fortunetelling, Forecasting, or Divination?

The primary difference among these three is semantics.

They are basically one and the same: you draw cards, interpret them, and make predictions based on the patterns you see.

The word "fortunetelling" has a bad rep, thanks in part to the media's depiction of card readers as your standard New Age weirdos. Somehow, the word "divination" has loftier connotations, probably because of its derivation from the word "divine." The term "forecasting," however, is the most respectable of the three. Forecasters, after all, are the people who tell us where a hurricane might hit, what stocks will be hot, what future trends will be.

The truth is that regardless of which term you prefer, we're all curious about what tomorrow may bring. The tarot itself may not give you names or dates. But like weather forecasters, the tarot alerts you to the patterns in the past that have influenced patterns in the present, and it pinpoints patterns which may be operating in the future.

Suppose the key card in a particular reading is the Fool. All of us have experienced his wild enthusiasm, those magical moments when we leap into something with such unbridled glee that we don't worry about the consequences. The Fool is what Abraham Maslow, the father of humanistic psychology, might refer to as a peak moment, a brief but intense euphoria that rises from the knowledge that we are all connected to something larger and more vast than we had supposed. The Fool is evidence of David Bohm's implicate order. He is the three little pigs on their way out into the world. He is Pocahontas when she sings about the color of the wind. He is us when we were eighteen and believed we owned the world. He is us at thirty-five or fifty or seventy, empowered by his eagerness to embrace the next phase of the journey, whatever it will be.

As a key card in a spread, the Fool says you're about to embark on a magnificent journey in which time literally has no meaning at all. It can be a physical or a metaphorical journey; it might be a love affair. It might be as simple as glimpsing a splendid rainbow in the sky some evening and being so filled with wonder that the emotion spills over into the rest of your life. The Fool is archetypal, his history is as old as man.

Snapshots and Stories

The definitions of the majors are easy to remember; think of them as snapshots of our individual and collective journey. The trick is to piece them together into a story, to find the thread that connects them.

It's not enough to tell someone that he or she is about to go through some heavy changes. You have to be able to tell the person something about those changes and how they will impact his or her life.

This is where the majors are extremely helpful. A single major, as in the example of our neighbor's son, provides an intimate, piercing glimpse of someone else's life. It might take several spreads of minors to glean the same information.

And yet, without minor arcana cards, all we had was this single piercing glimpse of the truth: our neighbor was definitely pregnant. Several minor arcana cards might have told us whether the pregnancy was going to be easy or difficult; how it might affect the structure of her family; even whether she would have the same obstetrician for the entire pregnancy.

The majors and minors work together, as a democratic whole. It's through this cooperative spirit that they tap David Bohm's implicate order and enable the reader to interpret the pattern and tell a story.

Self-knowledge

Integral to your work with the tarot is the quest for self-knowledge, which empowers you.

To learn the cards, you have to read first for yourself. When you do that often enough, you begin to notice that certain cards keep coming up. These are the patterns that are probably prevalent in your life *at that moment.*

Let's suppose the three cards that appear most frequently over a period of several days or weeks are the eight of cups, the Hierophant, and the ten of swords. The first card talks about walking away from something that is finished. It is a conscious decision to turn away from a person or a situation that no longer satisfies your needs.

The second card addresses established organizations or structures: religion, family, court, hospital, corporation, anything that exists within strictly defined parameters. The third card also concerns endings, but in this instance it seems to be thrust upon you from an external source. It spells the end of a cycle.

But how do you put this together? What is the pattern depicted by these three cards? One possible interpretation might be that you keep encountering challenges with mainstream belief systems. You want to walk away from your church or your marriage or the company you work for, but you can't seem to muster the courage to do so on your own. So circumstances take care of it for you: your religious beliefs prove to be flawed, your spouse walks out, you're fired from your job. This doesn't happen just once, it happens repeatedly. The situations may vary, but the *pattern* is the same.

So you begin to ask yourself how you can *change* this pattern and improve your life. You take the first step into self-knowledge and empowerment. As you become more proficient with the cards, you begin to read for other people. By reading for others, your self-knowledge expands. Self-knowledge and empowerment are intrinsic to the tarot.

Maslow has a term for our search for who we are: self-actualization. The more conscious we are, the more clearly we perceive how we can reach our full potential. The clearer something appears to us, the better equipped we are to change the behaviors and patterns that block the attainment of what we want.

Tarot is a tool through which we experience Bohm's implicate order. It is synchronicity in its purest form, the visual depiction of Jung's collective unconscious. It is you, turned inside out.

Use it wisely.

3

The Major Arcana

Since the majors concern significant issues in our lives rather than daily occurrences, their importance prevails over all other cards in the deck. The majors are particularly rich and multilayered in their meanings, so the deck you use will be especially important. The more the artwork resonates for you, the better you'll be able to interpret and explain the trumps to the querent.

The majors should be the first group of cards in the deck with which you become familiar. The simplest way to learn their meanings is to pull a card or two at the beginning of your day and note them in your tarot journal. At the end of the day, compare their meanings to what actually happened during the day. Pay special attention to any cards that turn up repeatedly; they indicate a pattern that needs to be addressed.

Combinations

In a reading for yourself or someone else, try to interpret the cards in combinations by drawing correlations among them. It's rather like following the plotline in a story. What's the tension? Who are the players? What are the events that come into play? What is the probable resolution?

Janice, a publicist for a publishing house, wanted to know the outlook for leaving her job and moving to another city to go to school. She drew four cards: the Empress, Death, the World, and the Lovers.

The first card, the reason for asking, indicated that the time for such a move was fertile. This was something she needed to do to nurture new aspects of herself.

The Death card, what she needed to know about the pending decision, indicated that if she decided to leave her job, she would be shutting the door for good on that part of her life—and probably on publicity as a career. She wasn't entirely convinced she wanted to do that.

Regardless of what she decided, she would inherit the World. If she remained, it might mean a promotion and a raise. If she left, the move would open new doors in her life, bring new opportunities and social contacts. It would prove extremely successful for her.

The last card, the Lovers, was the outcome. Since she wasn't seriously involved with anyone at this point, the appearance of this card seemed to indicate that ultimately it would come down to a choice for her: whether to stay or leave.

Eight months after this reading, she was still at the publishing house. But she had been promoted and loved every facet of her work.

Keep in mind that when you do a reading with just the majors, it's a good idea to draw an equal number of minor arcana cards and read them in conjunction with the majors they cover. This gives you a concise picture of how the energy of each of the majors will manifest and who or what situations and events will be involved.

The Fool—Key 0

He represents the unlimited potential of the human spirit, purity of action untouched by experience. The Fool is no fool, but an innocent who embraces whatever life brings. His open mind, the simplicity of his motives, and his sheer exuberance leave no room for doubt or fear. He possesses the imagination, creativity, and innate wisdom of a child, and like a child, he rushes forward without hesitation. He trusts his instincts.

Depending on where he falls in a spread, the Fool may also indicate that you're pushing too far, too fast. You may be acting in an unrealistic or irresponsible manner. The magnificent exuberance that makes you feel like you're eighteen again may irritate the people who are closest to you.

IN A READING: A fresh start or new beginning. Expect the unexpected. You take risks that shock the people who know you best, but you're indifferent to their criticisms. You believe that all things are possible if you trust your instincts, plunge ahead, and don't worry about consequences. The Fool is definitely right-brained.

WORK: You start a new project, find a new job, embark on some glorious adventure. Travel is involved. Your enormous enthusiasm infects everyone around you and benefits you professionally.

ROMANCE: You're not ready to make a commitment, even though you may be pressured to do so. You're having too much fun to be tied down, you're too restless to stick to one person, starting a family is the farthest thing from your mind. You're living completely in the now. Life is immediate.

FINANCES: The check isn't in the mail, it has arrived. The mortgage or loan you've applied for is approved. New financial opportunities appear in your life. Expect increase. You enter a period of perfect faith; you know that no matter what happens, it's going to be okay.

HEALTH: Definite improvement. You plunge ahead despite your health problems and find exactly what you need in order to recover. This may entail alternative medicine, a holistic physician, or a spiritual awakening that dramatically affects your physical self. Remissions occur. However, you may be accident-prone or forgetful.

SPIRITUALITY: Your quest is underway. You're sampling everything that's out there—sweat lodges, fasting, past-life workshops, near-death seminars, religious or pagan rituals, tantric practices, out-of-body experiences, drugs, dreams, music. Everything you experience leads you to a deeper understanding of who you are and what you believe. The risks you take astonish the people who know you best. You've been seized, you must keep going.

EMPOWERMENT: Today is the first day of your life.

The Magician—Key 1

He is the protagonist of John Fowles's brilliant novel *The Magus*. He consciously creates reality through his will and imagination. As an alchemist and transformer, he epitomizes the ability to translate ideas into action. He relies on self-confidence, power, and determination to see him through. The astrological counterpart of the Magician is Mercury, the planet of mental agility and quickness. He symbolizes creative intelligence, psychic discovery, new beginnings, and the realization that with desire, intent, and focus, all our dreams are within our reach.

IN A READING: Seemingly magical influences come into your life and you intuit or invent solutions to your most pressing problems. You suddenly notice synchronicities that point to a deeper order and organization. You take the unconscious energy of the Fool, sculpt it, and direct it to create what you want and need.

WORK: Success is practically on top of you. You begin a new job, that promotion or bonus you've been hoping for comes through. Creative endeavors take off, your dreams and desires, whatever they are, materialize. Be cautious around associates who use trickery and manipulation to control others.

ROMANCE: A romantic partnership grows and flourishes or you meet someone new under unusual circumstances. The magic that attracted you to your significant other in the first place now seems to rise to newer, higher levels, and transforms the relationship. You divine each other's dreams, communicate telepathically. You've found a soul mate.

FINANCES: Your finances improve dramatically. A new enterprise substantially augments your earnings and provides a much-needed creative outlet. You get a break in your mortgage payments, are able to pay off your credit cards, and have money left over to sock away.

HEALTH: Problems clear up spontaneously. As shaman and healer, the Magician points the way to alternative medical care. Remember that illness is often a wake-up call; pinpoint what's missing from your life, then go after it. Listen to the wisdom of your body. A particular dietary change benefits you and it isn't just a phase; you incorporate it into your life.

SPIRITUALITY: Esoteric and metaphysical knowledge provide you with answers to your questions. You join a discussion group or study on your own. By opening yourself to the life-giving powers of creation, you draw them to you. Your teacher-guide offers aid and enlightenment and accompanies you on your path.

EMPOWERMENT: Conscious magic provides the power and energy to change your life.

The High Priestess—Key 2

Think virgin goddess, daughter of the moon, archetype of feminine consciousness. She is intuition and inspiration. Her wisdom burns from within, she plies her craft in secrecy. Her knowledge resides in the heart. Passive and receptive, she guards the gate of the unconscious and connects you to dreams, psychic powers, lunar cycles, menstruation, female mysteries.

Her astrological sign is Cancer, her element is water, and her number is two, which represents balance. The High Priestess knows but doesn't tell. She prompts us to look deep inside ourselves and seek our own answers.

IN A READING: Something is hidden in your life, a mystery or a secret eludes you. The answer may be found in your memories or dreams of the past. Rely more on intuition than intellect. Remain open to information that flows from your unconscious.

The high priestess may represent a mysterious woman in a man's life, a femme fatale, sexual and charismatic, who remains aloof and detached from emotional involvement. In a woman's life, she represents intuition.

WORK: Things may be slow for a while, but a surprise seizes you—a bonus, a pay raise, perhaps even a promotion or a new job opportunity. A woman in your work environment loves to gossip, but reveals nothing about herself. You come up with a new way of doing something that increases your efficiency and saves you time.

ROMANCE: Your significant other isn't telling you everything. She's remote, cool, wrapped up in her own affairs, so you play the waiting game. Your detachment about romance in general allows you to direct your energy into other areas of your life. Follow your inner voice.

FINANCES: You don't have the full story and a woman figures prominently in what you don't know. She may be a Scorpio or someone with Scorpio attributes: secretive, sexual, sly, psychic, vindictive. Probe beneath the surface, ask questions, do your own snooping, keep your own counsel.

HEALTH: Accept nothing at face value. You don't have all the information you need to make a decision about your treatment. Question the diagnosis, the tests, your physician. If the traditional treatment for what ails you doesn't feel right at a gut level, don't go through with it. Listen to your body, heed your dreams, be aware of synchronicities that pertain to your health. Request a healing dream.

SPIRITUALITY: Your personal path may still be hidden or unclear. But by remaining open and receptive to cues in your daily life, you attain the understanding you need.

EMPOWERMENT: Draw on your mystique and your intuition to achieve what you want.

The Empress—Key 3

She's the Great Mother Goddess in her guise as Ceres/ Demeter, who created the seasons as a symbol of the ebb and flow of all human life. As Mother Nature, she governs the cycle of birth, death, and rebirth. She sets our world in order and grants us the cornucopia of Earth's bounty.

She represents fertility, practicality, good luck, and success. Her intuition and insight crosses genders. Her domain lies in emotions, feelings, inner promptings. In astrology, her mate is Venus, the embodiment of emotional love, sensual pleasure, and sexual passion.

IN A READING: Your life swells with abundance. You're a nurturer who takes in strays, eases other people's pain, and soothes their anxieties. Your openness and receptivity make you a good listener and an excellent counselor. Your home is warm, inviting, and filled with good food. It's also your sanctuary, your sacred place. The Empress often refers to your own mother or someone with maternal traits.

WORK: Ideas blossom. Your plans find the support they need and because they speak to other people, they succeed. You open a day care center, work at the local animal shelter, teach small children. Your work may well be your children. You inspire the lives you touch.

ROMANCE: It's a fertile time for affairs of the heart. Your timing is impeccable, synchronicities proliferate, you're swept up in the sensuous passion of a relationship. Nurture the relationship, but don't mother your significant other.

FINANCES: It's a good time for investments. Buy that piece of property or that house you've had your eye on. The check really *is* in the mail, that raise you've been hoping for comes through, your debt is consolidated, financial obligations ease up. By embracing the practical aspects of everyday life, prosperity finds you.

HEALTH: Pregnancy is a distinct possibility. If you're already pregnant, expect an easy nine months and an uncomplicated labor and delivery unless surrounding cards indicate otherwise. Your emotional satisfaction lies in anything having to do with your children, family, and creative projects. This satisfaction, in turn, has a positive affect on your health. You benefit from gardening, by being surrounded by bright flowers, trees. Even a day at the beach revitalizes you. Take time to nurture *yourself.*

SPIRITUALITY: You're spiritually energized by nurturing all facets of your home environment. Answers that you need are found serendipitously through family and children, animals and nature, books and art. Cultivate your fantasies and dreams, dare to reach for all that you imagine.

EMPOWERMENT: Nurture all that you are, so that you become all that you can be.

The Emperor—Key 4

He represents the order in our lives, the authority figures: bosses, fathers, government, police, courts, and society in general. He's about logic, reasoning, left-brain thinking, solidity, foundations. Part of the Emperor's work is to organize clusters of our root beliefs into conscious frameworks.

His astrological cohort is Aries the Ram, a sign of leadership and energy. He draws his energy from fire and governs action, war, conquest, and victory.

IN A READING: Something you desire is starting to appear in your life, even if you can't see it yet. Your greatest strength is the power of your will. You view every obstacle as a challenge. Through visualization and affirmations, you make your intention and desires clear and the universe responds. The more focused your intent, the faster the manifestation. Don't be obnoxious about what you're striving for; others may not see things as you do.

WORK: You put plans into action and carry them out successfully. Your organizational abilities are noticed by an older man, perhaps a boss, who commends you for a job well done. He may be somewhat dictatorial, but you can learn from him by listening and observing. You get the raise and promotion you deserve and find your career niche, the spot where you can make a difference.

ROMANCE: Your significant other is older than you, left-brained, confident, probably opinionated. He or she may be your boss, a coworker, or someone you meet through your job. The chemistry may not be immediate, but it grows. The two of you create a private little kingdom where your diverse opinions flourish.

FINANCES: You don't just start earning more money, you *create* financial opportunities through your focused intent. Be alert for synchronicities, then pursue them, see where they lead. Follow your impulses. Your higher self knows that money is simply energy and leads you to people and opportunities that increase your finances.

HEALTH: You follow traditional treatments and therapies. Your physician may not have much of a bedside manner, but you believe in his ability to heal you. Although you supplement his therapy with vitamins, you do it on the sly because you don't want to incur his disapproval. Belief in your right to good health helps more than any therapy you undergo.

SPIRITUALITY: Your left-brain interests and intellectual passions lead you into the total, right-brain picture. You attain a kind of peace about where you are and where you want to be. Carve out your personal spiritual space—an altar, a wishboard, or just time for yourself.

EMPOWERMENT: Through focused intent, you create the conditions conducive to finding and realizing your heart's desire, whatever it may be.

The Hierophant—Key 5

Organizations, groups, and structures are represented by this card: religion, family, corporate America. It's about tradition, ritual, the established way of doing things. It is yang, masculine. Its astrological association is Jupiter, which in astrology rules the ninth house of higher education, organized religion, and theological leaders.

IN A READING: You come up against the powers that be— whether religious, corporate, or family. This clash of belief systems helps you clarify your own position. A counselor, pastor, teacher, or parent offers orthodox advice or guidance that drives you nuts. Ultimately, you make your own decision and find a way to incorporate your ideas into the existing structure.

WORK: Your professional life is centered within a traditional, organized system. Success comes through following the rules and sticking with work methods that have proven successful. By aligning yourself with the powers that be, you move ahead more quickly. But don't compromise your personal integrity just to avoid expressing what may be a differing opinion.

ROMANCE: A marriage may be in the offing, a traditional church wedding versus a ten-minute ceremony in Las Vegas. If you've recently met someone, the relationship is steeped in convention—the man does the courting and the woman waits by the phone. If you try to reverse the roles, the relationship backfires. The relationship conforms to society's expectations.

FINANCES: Stable, down-to-earth strategies are highlighted. Seek the advice of orthodox investment counselors. Stash your savings in an IRA or Keogh, where you won't be tempted to touch it, or invest in land or a home. Your long-term financial outlook is bright, but you have to follow the rules.

HEALTH: Seek the aid of ritualized therapy. This may be conventional medicine, with the gamut of medical tests— MRIs, CAT scans, blood work—or it may be alternative therapies. Whichever path you choose, the point is the rite, the regularity, your commitment. Paramount to healing is your belief in your body's ability to heal and in your own power to attract the healer you need.

SPIRITUAL: You benefit from tradition. Conventional belief systems challenge you and deepen your spiritual values. Take time to connect with your spiritual self, whether it's through meditation, prayer, or just a ceremonial homage to nature. Ceremony becomes your gateway to higher knowledge. The key is commitment to daily exploration of a particular path.

EMPOWERMENT: Ritual energizes you and connects you to the source of All That Is.

The Lovers—Key 6

This card is about choices, duality, and decisions that sometimes concern a love affair. It points to sudden and unexpected changes in a relationship, adjustments in your love life that work in your favor, a choice between security and some sort of personal risk.

Part of the Lovers' work is to make us aware of the duality of our own natures and how it affects our close personal relationships. It's associated with the sign of Gemini, the twins of the zodiac.

IN A READING: A new relationship is just around the corner or a current relationship is about to go through big changes. You feel divided about a major issue or relationship in your life. Your heart whispers one tale, your head screams another.

WORK: You're facing a decision, and once you make it, expect improvement in your work/career. Something that looks negative on the surface turns out to be a blessing in disguise. You're charmed by someone you work with and feel conflicted about taking the relationship any further. Go with what feels right.

ROMANCE: Decision time. The relationship you're involved in is going through a tense, bumpy period. You or your significant other feel attracted to someone else but don't know how to verbalize it. You would like to ignore the situation and hope it goes away. Avoid confrontation. Attempt a gentle but honest discussion. Paired with the High Priestess or a court card, it often points to something hidden in a relationship—an extramarital affair or secrets that need to come out into the open. Someone—a family member, friend, or coworker—is interfering in your marriage or relationship.

FINANCES: Burdens ease once you make a decision about something that affects your pocketbook. Money comes through cooperation, partnership, or the bringing together of a coalition of forces working for a common goal. Now is the right time for you and your significant other to go into business together.

HEALTH: You must decide whether to go through medical tests or changes in lifestyle. Get a second opinion on any diagnosis. Try out various therapies, both conventional and alternative. Use visualizations and affirmations. Probe to understand your core beliefs about health, illness, and the body's integrity.

SPIRITUALITY: Gain through travel to exotic, mysterious locations. Sample weekend seminars and workshops on the practical application of metaphysics. Past life information helps heal a spiritual malaise.

EMPOWERMENT: Decide. And then move on, secure in the knowledge that your choice is the right one.

The Chariot—Key 7

It exemplifies the hero's journey and represents ambition, determination, and youthful energy. Its charioteer harnesses his power and talents and forges ahead, driven by a burning desire to succeed. Like Indiana Jones, the charioteer succeeds through a combination of self-discipline, bravado, and sheer willpower.

This is the "go for it" card and its purpose is to inspire you to test what you have learned and to prove your abilities. Unlike the Fool, the individual who drives the Chariot knows the reason for his journey.

IN A READING: A journey. It can be a spiritual journey of self-discovery or an actual trip, usually by car. Either way, you're in the driver's seat and you create your own destiny through your actions. A new car is a distinct possibility. You may move to another house or apartment within the same general area where you now live.

WORK: A project you've been working on for some time now reaches fruition. This happens in spite of your boss, who is being unreasonable. His agenda differs from yours and you simply work around it rather than trying to convert him to your way of thinking. Test what you've learned, prove your abilities, focus on your goals, and don't be discouraged by apparent obstacles.

ROMANCE: You have little time or inclination for romance. You're out for a good time and open to a fast fling; emotional involvement isn't part of your present plan. You may take off for a weekend with someone you're seeing, but you're more interested in the place you visit than the person you're with.

FINANCES: You spend money on a car either by fixing up the vehicle you have or buying a new one. Your bank offers an excellent deal on financing a new car at a reasonable interest rate. You're able to pay off outstanding credit card debts and can finally see your way clear to saving some of what you earn.

HEALTH: Preventive medicine is the key word. Work out to stay in shape, watch your diet, avoid overexertion. Your nerves may be vulnerable, so when you're tired or don't feel well, take it easy, slow down. A chronic health problem improves significantly and part of it is due to the fact that you're too busy with other things to obsess about it.

SPIRITUALITY: You embark on a journey of self-discovery. It involves workshops, seminars, travel to power spots. You are starting to open psychically—through dreams, clairvoyant impressions, perhaps through clairaudience. You find the appropriate tools to enhance your burgeoning psychic abilities.

EMPOWERMENT: Through purposeful action, you achieve your goals.

Strength—Key 8

The astrological counterpart of Strength is Leo the lion, which stands for rulership. The rulership implied in this card is one of self-dominion and implicit trust in your own abilities. A strong person doesn't need to exercise control over others. This strength comes from within and is based on wisdom, knowledge, and the belief that you have in yourself.

While the confidence of the Chariot is the male archetype of raw courage, the confidence of Strength lies in the female archetype of internal power. Strength implies a balance between the spiritual and material and harmony between opposing forces. Instead of fighting the beast, you tame it inside yourself.

IN A READING: You have the innate ability to deal with whatever life brings. Draw on your enormous energy to break through and overcome obstacles. You seize control of your own destiny and move forward with your plans. By cultivating inner fortitude, you attract the contacts and opportunities you need.

WORK: You're in a strong position. Request a raise, a promotion, whatever you feel you deserve. Your coworkers look to you for guidance. Forge ahead on your career plans. Patience and endurance pay off. You do what you need to do, then slip away before the hoopla begins.

ROMANCE: Your libido sizzles, your sex life takes off. You meet someone to whom you're instantly attracted and enter into a passionate affair. If you're already involved with someone, the relationship leaps into a passionate, intense period. You feel confident and strong in this relationship; you don't compromise your integrity just to keep the peace.

FINANCES: Debts are paid, the money you've been expecting arrives. Be patient but firm in financial dealings with people who owe you money. You move ahead with your financial plans, which may include buying a home or property.

HEALTH: The medical tests come back negative, your health takes a dramatic turn for the better. Capitalize on it by correcting bad dietary and lifestyle habits. Start an exercise regimen. Take ten or fifteen minutes a day to meditate, to fully relax into the moment. Start keeping a journal; you'll benefit by putting your thoughts on paper, where you can see them.

SPIRITUALITY: You find the right balance between the spiritual and the material. You're able to successfully blend your conscious and unconscious powers. Listen to your intuition and call on your inner knowing to help you manifest whatever you want.

EMPOWERMENT: Willpower and determination conquer obstacles.

Hermit—Key 9

Envision Diogenes searching for the truth. His journey is solitary, self-contained, the path of the true seeker. One way or another, the Hermit finds the answers to his questions, solves his problems, completes his projects.

He symbolizes the deeper levels of the psyche, the wisdom of the higher self. He often represents a teacher of hidden things, spiritual matters, occult secrets, someone whose inner light illuminates the lives of others. This card is connected to Saturn or Cronus and relates to the astrological Saturn Return that occurs approximately once every twenty-eight years. Like Saturn, the Hermit is a taskmaster and tester; he forces us to get serious about our lives.

IN A READING: The period of solitude you've been in is nearing completion. Tie up loose ends, finish projects, and plan ahead for the next phase. You attend workshops, lectures, and take courses that help you achieve your goals. This can include returning to college or enrolling in graduate school after a long hiatus. Travel is related to metaphysics and education.

WORK: You reach a crossroads; take a step back and reexamine your situation. Things have been slow, but now you experience an increase in productivity. Emphasize time management, research, planning, instruction. Success and recognition are within your reach.

ROMANCE: Having retreated into yourself, relationships are not currently a priority in your life. In spite of feelings of detachment, you will connect with someone soon. A romance is rekindled or a person you regard as a mentor or guide becomes something more.

FINANCES: You're not overly concerned about money or tangible assets. If unexpected money comes your way, great, but don't waste it. Buy a CD or a stock with a good track record. Invest in a money market. Put the money in something that agrees with your beliefs. You benefit financially from metaphysics, study, teaching, and solitary pursuits.

HEALTH: Your health complaints are the physical manifestation of your search for the truth. Examine your health problems as metaphors for work you need to do in particular areas of your life. A muscular stiffness, for instance, may indicate a need to loosen up your beliefs regarding certain topic. If your allergies act up, ask who you're allergic to.

SPIRITUALITY: Blessed with the ability to teach and enlighten, you realize that you don't have all the answers. You are at once student and teacher. During this time of introversion and spiritual seeking, learn to listen with your inner ear and your own truths will surface.

EMPOWERMENT: You reemerge refreshed from this period of solitude and inner focus.

The Wheel of Fortune—Key 10

The wheel of life reveals our connection to luck and destiny. You don't have to remain locked in place. Embrace the risk, take the plunge, and luck rides with you. Once you've set everything in motion, the universe responds quickly to your desires.

Sudden, unexpected changes connect this card to the planet Uranus. Originality and unconventional ideas trigger new methods, new lifestyles, and new belief systems. Revolutionize your lifestyle and bring it more in line with who you are or who you want to be.

IN A READING: You've reached a turning point in your life. The hub of the wheel relates to stability, but the outer rim portends change, taking a gamble. Take your cues from unexpected events and synchronicities; the fates are trying to coax you in a new direction. Although you're free to resist, you profit by going with the flow, whatever it is.

WORK: You enter a new work cycle, which may entail leaving your current job to pursue your dream. Follow your intuition, don't let fear block your progress. Once you take the needed risk, things break wide open. You're the only person who is keeping you where you are. Once you realize this, you're liberated.

ROMANCE: Your timing has been off, you're stuck in a rut, spinning your wheels. An old relationship no longer meets your needs; release it or reevaluate it. If you're not involved, pinpoint the attributes you're looking for. Then take a risk— accept that blind date, meet new friends for dinner. Don't sit around feeling sorry for yourself. The person you meet reflects the new you.

FINANCES: You're on a roll, so trust your gut. Don't get stuck in a holding pattern. Sell off properties, stocks, and bonds that haven't performed as well as you hoped. Invest in growth stocks and new products. Take a personal risk: set up your own business, go into partnership with an innovative individual, bank on your own creativity.

HEALTH: Suppressed emotions and resistance to change cause emotional and mental imbalances. Open up, speak your mind, defend whatever it is you believe in. Be yourself. Be flexible, stretch, move, exercise, breathe. You benefit from yoga, aerobics, swimming, a regular exercise routine. Get rid of outdated eating habits. Do some research, sample nutritional advances, then decide what's best for you.

SPIRITUALITY: You've reached the point where you realize there is more to you and your life than the external world (the outer rim of the wheel). Commune with your inner self (the wheel's hub) and discover the core of strength from which you create your worldly fortune.

EMPOWERMENT: Your own thoughts and beliefs turn the wheel; take responsibility for your actions.

Justice—Key 11

The astrological counterpart of Justice is Libra, the scales. The double-edged sword depicted in most versions of this card represents choice and indicates that Justice is a two-way street. The scales refer to balance and harmony. The type of justice represented is legal or karmic justice, not social justice, which is in the realm of the Emperor.

Its influence is impartial, objective, detached, and non-judgmental. Compromise is intrinsic to this card—learning to do what's necessary in order to be fair to ourselves and others. The balanced personality has few preconceptions or prejudices. When decisions need to be made, you must learn to weigh all factors in order to render an equitable decision.

IN A READING: Your legal problems wane; a judgment is in your favor. However, your daily life activity may be suspended until a judgment is reached. What you've waited for materializes, conflicts are resolved, harmony reigns. You get what you believe you deserve and experience the world as an echo of your own thoughts and actions. When you deal fairly with others in good conscience, you receive a fair deal in return.

WORK: You need to bring your life into balance by rearranging your priorities. By overemphasizing your career, your home life suffers; the reverse is also true. Look at both sides of an issue and weigh all factors before making a decision. Focus on your goals in order to create a clear picture of what you want to accomplish, then go for it!

ROMANCE: One cycle ends and another begins. Contracts are made or broken—in other words, marriage, legal separation, or divorce. Concentrate on the quality, not the quantity, of future relationships. Remain firm in your convictions, whatever they are, and your heart's desire is obtained much more quickly.

FINANCES: A contract arrives in the mail, a legal judgment is in your favor, you make the deal you've been waiting for. The financial darkness you've been facing is suddenly illumined; you can see your way clear. An unexpected windfall shows up just in time to tide you over.

HEALTH: Balance, balance, balance! Are you eating too much, working too hard, not getting enough exercise or sleep? By allowing yourself to flow with the cycles of nature, you improve your health and sense of well-being. Take a long walk in the woods, by a beach, under a hot sun. You benefit immeasurably by living in the now.

SPIRITUALITY: As you begin to understand your place in the scheme of things, you feel your connection to All That Is. When you are centered and grounded, you experience what it means to "be here now."

EMPOWERMENT: You are between cycles, yesterday is gone and tomorrow is not yet here. Enjoy today.

The Hanged Man—Key 12

Think transition, postponed plans, a life in suspension, stagnation, and frustration. You need to do a one-eighty in how you perceive something. After all, a person hanging upside down doesn't see the world in the same way as someone standing on the ground.

This marks the point in the Fool's journey when he begins to question the deeper meaning and purpose of his life. The old beliefs and ideas have lost their meaning and no longer satisfy him, but he is confused about his new direction. The Hanged Man is the nonconformist of the Major Arcana. Unresponsive to anyone else's opinion, he goes his own way and does what he thinks is best.

IN A READING: Adjust your point of view, reverse your established order of doing things. The decision you're waiting for is delayed. Make an effort to avoid victim consciousness; this standstill isn't permanent. You're stuck in a rut because of rigid ideas and fixed concepts. If no one seems to agree with you it may be because others have moved on and you have not. Release ideas and associations that are obsolete.

WORK: There won't be any immediate word on your promotion or raise. Negotiations are stalled, you're tired of waiting. But resist the temptation to play the martyr. This impasse is only temporary, conditions will improve soon.

ROMANCE: Your current relationship appears to be stuck in neutral. Try looking at the situation from your partner's point of view. Once you do, an answer that has eluded you becomes utterly clear. Your feelings of loneliness and isolation are only temporary.

FINANCES: The check isn't in the mail, the stock you bought last week hasn't gone up, your bank account isn't getting any fatter. But once you change your perspective on these issues, the block is broken and everything begins to move forward again. The impetus may be something as simple as defining the parameters of what you can and can't live with.

HEALTH: You undergo a complete reversal in your ideas regarding a long-term health problem. Try a new approach, change doctors if necessary. Research alternative treatment and therapy. Your dis-ease improves step-by-step.

SPIRITUALITY: Events in your life force you to look within. You realize, perhaps for the first time, that the inner reality creates the outer reality. One is the direct reflection of the other. Change what you believe and your life changes accordingly. Dare to begin your inner journey even if it involves some risk or sacrifice.

EMPOWERMENT: Turn your life around by letting go of (sacrificing) negative beliefs.

Death—Key 13

Don't panic: The Death card doesn't mean physical death. It's about transition, transformation, rebirth, and permanent change. This revitalizing force sweeps away the old to make way for the new. The change symbolized by Death is permanent: You go through a door and it slams shut behind you forever. The astrological correspondence is Scorpio and the eighth house of death and regeneration.

Comparable to the Tower, this card indicates that change is required. If you don't change willingly, something will slam into your life that forces you to change. Then, like the phoenix, you rise reborn from the ashes of your old life.

IN A READING: Are you afraid of the future? Do you have a compulsion to cling to old situations no matter what the cost? If so, then expect a complete turnaround. Superficial changes aren't enough now; the old situation must be turned inside out. The devastating changes you experience seem so hopeless you nearly surrender to despair. Then, quite suddenly, your situation improves. You can breathe again.

WORK: You lose the job that you dislike, but which you've been unwilling to leave because of the steady income. Use this as an opportunity to seek out a new occupation or career, even if means going back to school. Ultimately, you benefit from the loss of your job.

ROMANCE: You end the relationship that you have long since outgrown but have been afraid to leave. Letting go of the familiar may be extremely painful, but it helps you clarify what you're looking for in a partner. In the end, you find a happier, more fulfilling union.

FINANCES: Loss of capital or income is possible. Your company downsizes. Your stocks drop. You have trouble paying your bills or making ends meet. The bank forecloses on your house. You're forced to make difficult decisions and to move in a new direction. Then you recoup your losses and profit from what you've learned.

HEALTH: Physical symptoms and conditions associated with this card are: constipation (a resistance to "letting go" of old habits); root canals (a signal that root beliefs are changing); surgeries (a need to "cut free" from certain restrictive situations). Don't fight the tide. Roll with it, take care of problems as they arise, and recognize these irritating problems for what they are: a call from your inner self to pay attention.

SPIRITUALITY: Transformation occurs as you release situations and relationships that no longer serve your purpose. You become who you really are rather than who you think you ought to be. That's the true meaning of dying in order to be reborn.

EMPOWERMENT: Transformation and metamorphosis awaken you to your own immortality.

Temperance—Key 14

In some decks, this card is called the Alchemist. It usually depicts an angel standing with one foot in the water and the other on earth, indicating that the temperate personality links the realms of the conscious and the unconscious.

The word temperance comes from the Latin *temperare* and means to mix or combine properly. The card itself indicates a need to mix and match until you find what is right for you.

IN A READING: Tranquility comes to you through your ability to maintain harmony and balance by the successful blending of opposites. You're learning to temper justice with compassion, success with failure, joy with sorrow. Moderation in all things is required. Compromise and tolerance for opinions different from your own take you a long way. This doesn't mean you must surrender yourself to someone else's agenda.

WORK: Look for a new way of doing an old job. Create a calm and relaxed work atmosphere so that stressful tasks can be accomplished with ease. Success won't be instantaneous, but your patience and perseverance pay off. Your boss or a coworker can be trying at times; ignore it and go about your own business.

ROMANCE: Compassion, cooperation, and forgiveness create a bond with your significant other that has been absent lately. Calm, open discussion about your differences and complaints bring about the results you want. Listen to your feelings, look honestly at the facts, then act. If you're single, don't rush impulsively into a new relationship. Take time to get to know the person before you commit yourself to a deepening involvement.

FINANCES: Your patience has worn thin, you're tired of waiting for that raise or promotion or that winning lottery ticket. Negotiate with someone to get what you've earned. Maintain your composure and present your case in a simple, forthright manner.

HEALTH: Your physical problems act as a springboard for discovery—specifically that you possess the gift of healing. It may manifest through psychic healing or through more traditional medical training. You may also encounter this gift in another person and at precisely the time when you need it. Moderation improves your health.

SPIRITUALITY: The key to your personal path lies in harmony, peace, and focused attention on what you desire and need. Answers come to you through meditation, the practice of yoga, dreams. You experience a state of peaceful repose by grounding and channeling cosmic energies.

EMPOWERMENT: Balance and energy suffuse your life. You're in harmony with All That Is.

The Devil—Key 15

This card personifies temptation, burdens, restrictions, choices, and misdirection. It reflects belief in the surface rather than in the inner truth of a situation. Limits, boundaries, and being a slave to desires overpower innate good judgment.

The Devil represents your own fears; he is the path of least resistance. You believe that you can't do anything, that you're powerless to exert control over your life. In order to escape his bondage you must alter your thoughts and actions. It's time you realized that the chains that hold you can be removed at will.

IN A READING: Are you a passive chooser rather than an active chooser? If you let life's events make decisions for you, then you are passively choosing, trapped in inertia and feelings of helplessness. Take charge of your own life and "choose to choose." The Devil can be exorcised by changing the patterns of behavior or thinking that keep you in a master/slave situation.

WORK: Materialism and profit are the driving forces behind your ambition; you no longer seek satisfaction and deeper meaning in your work. Emphasis on money and/or fear prevent you from achieving what you really want. You or your boss may be a control freak. Your work conditions right now require you to punch a clock (either literally or figuratively) and you feel suffocated by all the rules.

ROMANCE: You may be intimately involved with a substance abuser and at times feel that *you* are chained to the substance as well. You know intuitively that you can't change the other person, but you continue in the relationship even though it threatens to drag you down. The powerful sexual chemistry between you and your significant other no longer compensates for what is lacking.

FINANCES: Temptation. Look closely at deals that promise big returns at the expense of the gullible, ignorant, or innocent. Don't abandon your principles and scruples in favor of material gain. Avoid going into business with your lover as long as the relationship skews your financial judgments.

HEALTH: You cling to your *dis-ease* even though it no longer serves as a springboard for growth. You can become run-down due to overwork or lack of sleep. Drugs and alcohol won't solve your problems. Mental depression may complicate your health difficulties. Instead of taking a prescription medicine, you benefit from physical exercise that gets you out of the house and out of your own head.

SPIRITUALITY: Your transformation begins the moment you affirm your intention to cast out negative energies and replace them with positive thoughts and actions.

EMPOWERMENT: Refuse to relinquish control of your own life.

The Tower—Key 16

This card symbolizes the breaking apart of structures that have kept you imprisoned. Sudden and unexpected life changes form the core of the Tower's meaning.

These changes seem to crash into your life out of nowhere. But if you're entirely honest with yourself about what you believe and the patterns you have set into motion in your life, you realize this card has appeared because of an inner urge to break free.

IN A READING: This is a wake-up call. A violent upheaval is in the offing. It may be something as weird as your house being struck by lightning or as unexpected and shattering as your spouse announcing that he or she is leaving. Even though this card portends surprising events, it's actually about sweeping your life clean.

Belief systems crumble, routines break down, and for a period of time you're adrift, in transition. Then new doors open, new chapters begin, and you're ushered into a new phase whether you're ready or not.

WORK: The news isn't good: A layoff may be in the wind. Don't be surprised if you're passed over for the promotion or raise you expected. The truth is that your current job or career isn't really where you want to spend the balance of your working life. You don't get the job you've applied for, your manuscript is rejected, your small business folds. Ultimately, the apparent tragedy places you squarely on the path you should be traveling.

ROMANCE: Stuck in a rut? A stifling relationship is about to end. If you're afraid to leave on your own, something unexpected happens that shoves you out of an unhappy situation. You flounder, loneliness plagues you. Then, suddenly, you place the events where they belong, your mood lifts, and you get on with your life.

FINANCES: The market plunges, funds for your projects are cut off, established companies go bankrupt, your loan application is rejected. You're forced to seek alternatives to what you want. Just when things look bleakest, however, serendipity rushes into your life. New and unexpected financial realms open to you.

HEALTH: Be careful! Watch out for car problems, fires or accidents around the home. Nervous disorder, tremors, high fevers, and bizarre symptoms cause concern. Surgery may be indicated. Your recovery is swift and complete.

SPIRITUALITY: Sudden enlightenment, the kind that surges from deep within, sweeps into your life. Something inexplicable occurs and your eyes are suddenly opened to the beauty of All That Is.

EMPOWERMENT: The overthrow of existing conditions brings new opportunity and a fresh start.

The Star—Key 17

Think balance and harmony and all things associated with Aquarius. In the wake of the Tower's violent eruption, you're inspired to reach for your highest potential. You experience order and peace. The Star guides you to your destination with the gentleness of her soft light.

This card is one of calm, renewal, and healing. A new cycle begins. Your persistence and hard work pay off big time. You experience a profound peace that springs from the unconscious. You're doing what you were born to do.

IN A READING: Everything works the way it should. Your life achieves wholeness, unity. Now you must show confidence and belief in your goals. Begin with a gesture that illustrates your belief, then work to refine the belief itself. What you're starting or planning today will reach far into the future. You're on the right track, your plans are about to bear fruit. Indecision and inner conflict are now resolved.

The more positive your outlook and plans, the better your prospect for success. The Star fulfills promises and brings good fortune in general.

WORK: If you're unhappy in your job, anticipate a turn for the better. Doors open. New opportunities come out of nowhere. Your manuscript sells, your script is optioned, your company goes public and the stock soars, your dream job literally lands in your lap. You attain your highest potential.

ROMANCE: Promising encounters loom on the horizon, someone special sails into your life, synchronicities run rampant. You provide or receive guidance about a relationship. You and your significant other renew your commitment to the relationship. What you thought was impossible now becomes possible.

FINANCES: Once you open yourself to the possibilities, your finances improve significantly. Investments grow, you've got more than you need to refurbish your home or build a new home. You have the means now to pay off outstanding debts. Everything works out better than you expected.

HEALTH: Chronic problems seem to clear up overnight, remission from a serious illness occurs, the miracle you've hoped for lights up your life. The alternative therapies you've pursued pay off. You benefit from retreats, spas, and time with the people you love the most. You finally acknowledge that the mind/body connection isn't just a theory, it's a fact.

SPIRITUALITY: You're linked to a higher plane, a more evolved vibration. You experience out-of-body travels, lucid dreams, a surge in unconscious activity. Give of yourself with compassion, through service. In doing so, you spread your wisdom and help others find the light.

EMPOWERMENT: When you wish upon a star your dreams come true.

The Moon—Key 18

You're carried into the labyrinth of the unconscious to the shadowy world of sleep and dreams. Under its spell, you enter the netherworld of illusion and mystery. The question here is: Will you surrender to fear and the dark night of the soul? If you embark on your journey with eagerness and courage, you may become a dream art scientist who gleans from dreams what is needed to improve waking life.

The Moon connects you to the mysteries and nurturing qualities of the female spirit, to emotions and intuitions, to the seduction and fear of the unknown. It sometimes indicates paranoia, but can also suggest actual deception, sabotage, even psychic attack.

IN A READING: You haven't been sleeping well; you may be worried about your family. Feelings of anxiety and insecurity haunt you. Someone that you thought you could count on has let you down, perhaps even deceived you. Mystery permeates your relationships. Face your fears in order to discover what is real and what is illusion.

Whatever you're going through is only a phase. Look to your dreams, daydreams, and intuitions for answers and solutions. Right now, logic and reason aren't as important as intuition and insight.

WORK: You probably don't know the full story or have all the facts. Mystery surrounds a work issue. Someone you work with isn't telling the whole truth about a situation. You're surrounded by women; a Cancer individual plays a prominent role in your working environment.

ROMANCE: Your relationships go through phases, some good, some bad. You work through disappointment and disillusionment in a current affair, but because of a deep, psychic attraction, you can't quite sever the tie. You and your significant other are coping with issues you've faced in previous lives.

FINANCES: Financial markets fluctuate. Don't cash in any investments that you purchased under mysterious circumstances. The loan you've applied for is delayed, your bank statements don't tally with your own figures. A female stockbroker or financial analyst offers a viable solution.

HEALTH: Have lumps or cysts biopsied. However, you are prone to psychic premonitions about your physical condition, so follow your intuition. If something doesn't feel right to you, don't do it. Get a second opinion and explore alternatives outside established medicine.

SPIRITUALITY: Your spiritual life deepens. You experience strange and lucid dreams, clairvoyance or clairaudience, astral projection, past-life flashes. Through dreams and meditation you enter the mysterious world of the psyche and experience its multidimensional reality.

EMPOWERMENT: Request help from your dreams to create your future.

The Sun—Key 19

This card is a portal, an opening in your life. It brings exuberance, enthusiasm, attainment, success, material wealth. All things associated with the sun are indicated: tropical climates, enlightenment, empowerment, and the joy of creativity and rebirth. This card's work is to cleanse, to purify, to enhance, to improve, to illuminate.

The Sun, like Leo, the sign it rules, deals with leadership and with being the center of attention. It's often indicative of adoration, arrogance, egotism, a self-centered personality. It can indicate an obsession with material success and a tendency to use others for your own gain.

IN A READING: You feel empowered because your goals seem clearer than they've ever been. You embrace your destiny and realize you've created it. By saying yes to opportunity, your life opens into new vistas. Be magnanimous and forgiving to other people. You can afford to be generous now that victory is assured.

You travel to a warm climate for business, pleasure, or both. This could be overseas travel to Mexico, Egypt, Greece, India, or Morocco. Your exploration may involve the awakening of a past-life memory associated with one of these places.

WORK: You get the job you applied for and it turns out to be everything you want. You love your work. Your productivity and creativity are recognized and appreciated. Travel associated with work takes you to a warm climate and may involve a workshop or seminar that is part work, part perk.

ROMANCE: If you're single, someone new captures your heart. You and your new love travel to the Caribbean or the Mediterranean. If you're already involved, you and your significant other experience a resurrection of earlier passion. Relax and enjoy yourself. You've earned it.

FINANCES: Luck tags your heels. Your earnings increase. Your raise or bank loan comes through. Your mortgage is approved. The stock you bought on a whim jumps in value. You treat yourself to a new computer or spend a small fortune on a dream vacation and love every minute of it.

HEALTH: You're in the wellness loop now. Your vitality is renewed, you feel emotional contentment, you make a rapid recovery from surgery or illness. Your recent physical complaints—a burning in your chest, irritating colds or flus—seem to vanish overnight. You've overcome your fears.

SPIRITUALITY: Sun consciousness represents the mind awakened from sleep. Free of the moon's illusions you view all of life as filled with truth and light.

EMPOWERMENT: You have survived the darkness. Now follow the light.

Judgement—Key 20

A spiritual awakening. By the time the Fool reaches this point in his journey, he has learned how to integrate his everyday awareness with higher consciousness. He now possesses all the qualities that he has been seeking on his pilgrimage: enlightenment, truth, hidden knowledge, and a sense of harmony and contentment. But because the journey moves in an upward spiral, the next time he passes this point he will be even wiser.

Wake up and realize your real work and path in life. Valuable lessons have been learned; now put them to practical use. You've been given a second chance and you're ready to live a more meaningful existence.

IN A READING: Release the past and start fresh. This means pay off old debts, take responsibility for your life, and stop blaming and judging others.

Happiness doesn't lie outside of yourself. Honestly review your past actions, consider how you have used or misused your opportunities, then envision your future as you wish it to be. Once you do this, your life changes for the better. The ideas that you hold firmly in your consciousness eventually appear in physical reality.

WORK: Showtime! Whatever you have been working on is put to the test. You're in line for a promotion; you come up with new, innovative ideas. A pending decision results in a green light for a project you've nurtured. Your manuscript sells, your customers multiply, your dream unfolds, you're in the driver's seat.

ROMANCE: Your relationships undergo a regeneration. You and your significant other either commit to make things work or call it quits. If you're uncommitted, you won't be for long, and the meeting is thick with synchronicities. Past-life memories surface when you meet this new individual.

FINANCES: Your earnings increase, contracts are in the mail or have just been signed. Problems arise from an unexpected difference of opinion over money or legal rights, but it's resolved in your favor. This could involve property boundaries, copyright issues, musical or dramatic rights. You may pay heavily for a speeding ticket, but you make a contact that somehow augments your earnings.

HEALTH: Be assured that regenerative healing powers are available to help you overcome dis-ease and dis-ability. The power pours through you when you need it most and transforms your ideas of what is possible. By releasing the past you also release the physical blockages that have caused you problems.

SPIRITUALITY: You're approaching a crossroads, a switch in belief systems. You're primed for a change of direction or purpose. Go with it.

EMPOWERMENT: You have the ability to transform yourself in order to create a new, better life.

The World—Key 21

With this card, the Fool's journey ends; he arrives at his destination. The goal has been reached and all the elements of a situation have been drawn into a synthesized whole.

You've reached a deep understanding of the issues that

concern you. You've begun to realize that everything in life starts within and radiates outward, that your most private beliefs create the reality that you live. Everything is available to you. Now it's time to free yourself from restriction. Expand your horizons.

IN A READING: Completion, success, fulfillment. You're ready to reap your rewards and move on to a new phase. If you've been working on a long-term project that seems like it will never end, be assured that the conclusion is near.

Don't assume that your ultimate goal in life has been attained. This card symbolizes peak experiences where you move a step closer toward becoming who you really are. This is an intermediate period in which you may enjoy your triumphs before you begin again as the Fool. The World dancer serves as a reminder that the journey is the true goal.

WORK: The focus is on international travel, foreign contacts, and world events that affect your business or profession. The foreign rights to your book sell, a movie producer options your work, your promotion surpasses your expectations. You're exactly where you want to be.

ROMANCE: You'll find what you're looking for in a romantic partnership. You may realize you've had it all the time. Travel proves beneficial to an existing relationship or brings someone new and exciting into your life. You may even move to your new partner's country.

FINANCES: If you draw this card when stagnation is the status quo, then take heart. Whatever you've been waiting for is nearly upon you. You suddenly acquire money, perhaps through an inheritance, and quite possibly from more than one source. Foreign investments pay off.

HEALTH: You find unity, harmony, and balance. It may come when you change from a conventional medical practitioner to someone who practices holistic medicine. Embrace synchronicities. They are your higher self's way of seizing your attention and guiding you to health practices that are more beneficial.

SPIRITUALITY: When you strike a balance between the physical and spiritual planes, you glimpse the deeper meaning and purpose of life's journey. By transcending the ordinary, even momentarily, you attain a measure of cosmic consciousness.

EMPOWERMENT: You have surmounted your obstacles and overcome your limitations.

4

Court Cards

Practicalities

The sixteen court cards in a typical tarot deck are the page, knight, queen, and king in each of the four suits. In nontraditional decks like Voyager and Motherpeace, they go by different names: daughter, son, priestess, shaman, or child, man, woman, sage. If you're just learning the tarot, using a nontraditional deck can be somewhat confusing.

But the problem with the court cards isn't what you call them; it's what they mean. In this sense, they are rather like the old TV show *What's My Line?* They are considered to represent people in our lives; qualities or actual events or even thoughts that we hold; or all of the above. The truth lies somewhere in between.

The best way to understand the court cards is through trial and error. This applies to all of the cards, but it's particularly important with the court cards. The surrounding cards also provide valuable insight about how a court card affects a question or issue.

If a woman is asking about her marriage and the five of cups turns up next to the court card that represents her, then it's likely she's grieving about the marriage. It's also likely that her husband has left her. If, on the other hand, the eight of cups turns up, then it's likely she has made a conscious decision to leave, that she's finished with the marriage and is ready to move on.

Reading for someone else is the easiest way to discover whether the court card meanings you have learned from books are meanings that work for you *in practice*. It also helps if you can determine before a reading how many people are involved in a specific question.

Suppose the person you're reading for is a married woman of at least thirty-five or forty years old who is having an affair with a married man of about the same age. If you know this before you begin the reading, then you'll be able to identify the court cards when they turn up in a reading. You won't waste time trying to determine who the kings and queens are and puzzling through their relationship to each other.

Who Is This Woman?

The significance of court cards varies greatly among tarot readers. Let's take the queen of cups as an example. The textbook meaning of this card is that she represents a kind, nurturing woman who is most probably a mother. She possesses highly developed intuition and may represent a clairvoyant, someone involved in metaphysics.

Rachel Pollack, in *78 Degrees of Wisdom*, describes the

queen of cups as someone who "joins consciousness to feeling. She knows what she wants and will take the steps necessary to get it. Yet she always acts with an awareness of love."

In *The Mythic Tarot*, the queen of cups is likened to Helen of Troy because she "embodies many of the deep and complex qualities which Helen appeared to possess. She is passionate, proud, and intense, refusing to bow to anyone," writes coauthor Juliet Sharman-Burke.

Rose Gwain, in her book *Discovering Your Self Through Tarot*, has this to say about the queen of cups: "A married queen of cups may not be committed to the marriage or to her job or to anything else she does. She may live in a vain and sensual fantasy world, always imagining possibilities for herself, but never doing anything to bring them about. As such she may be idle, manipulative, deceitful, and materialistic." Hardly a rave review.

James Wanless, creator of the *Voyager Tarot*, is far kinder. He calls her the woman of cups and says she is the "rejoicer . . . who feels and expresses the joy of life."

In *Choice-Centered Tarot*, Gail Fairfield refers to queens as "fulfilling"; she says they symbolize competency. She defines the queen of cups as "emotional or intuitive maturity."

So which definition is the right definition? It depends entirely on you.

For one friend of ours, a writer who had recently begun working with tarot, the queen of cups came to symbolize a character she was developing, a clairvoyant who also read cards. For another friend, the queen of cups represented her own mother. She can also be a boss, a mother-in-law, the other woman, an older sister, a wife, a relative. Or she may just represent qualities that you or someone close to you possesses.

The queen of cups turned up in a reading for Anna, a

young single woman who was facing difficult choices in a relationship. We described the attributes of the queen and asked if the description fit anyone currently in Anna's life, someone close to her.

There was a moment of awkward silence, then Anna explained that the man she was involved with was married and had two children. The queen symbolized the man's wife, which cast her appearance in the spread in an entirely different light.

Astrology and Court Cards

Many tarot readers associate the kings, queens, knights, and pages with certain astrological signs. We have included the most common assignations, but we don't recommend that you adhere to them too closely because it limits the possibilities in a reading. Besides, opinions vary about which court cards are associated with which astrological signs.

The twelve signs of the zodiac are broken down into four elements that represent certain types of energy. Fire symbolizes imagination and creativity (Aries, Leo, Sagittarius); air is mental and represents the intellect (Gemini, Libra, Aquarius); water represents feelings, emotions, intuition (Pisces, Cancer, Scorpio); and earth represents the body, material needs, corporeal existence (Taurus, Virgo, Capricorn). The suits of the minor arcana are built on a similar model: wands are fire; swords are air; cups are water; pentacles are earth.

When the queen of cups appears, she may or may not refer to a Scorpio woman in your life or in the life of the person for whom you're reading. But the chances are quite good that she refers to a nurturing, compassionate, and intuitive woman born under a water sign.

Court Cards as Significators

KINGS AND QUEENS

A significator is a card that symbolizes whomever you're reading for. If you choose the significator before you start the reading, it can be based on the person's skin and hair color, astrological sign, and/or age. Generally, a king represents a man and a queen, a woman. But genders can be tricky.

Quite often in a reading, a queen will turn up that symbolizes qualities and characteristics rather than gender. A man may have compassionate, nurturing qualities that are usually attributed to a woman (the queen of cups). Sometimes a man might choose a queen as a significator because the qualities of that particular queen are qualities he hopes to develop in himself.

Age, like gender, can also be a tricky. While a king usually represents a mature man, there are differing opinions about how old he is. We've found the king is almost always older than the querent, but to assign absolute parameters to his age is restrictive. If you say he's older than forty, but in the life of the person for whom you're reading the man represents someone who is in his late thirties, then he might be dismissed as a possibility. So be flexible about the age of the king.

To some degree this is also true of the queen. Her age span is wider than the king's—and she may be as young as twenty-five. Like the king, she is mature, but maturity varies from one individual to another. Again, be flexible and learn from experience. In time, you'll develop an intuitive sense about the specifics of these cards.

Some readers assign certain physical characteristics to the kings and queens. The queen of pentacles, for example, is described as a dark-skinned woman, possibly a foreigner, an earth sign with an excellent business sense. But to adhere too closely to this description can limit your interpretation of the cards.

In one six-month reading, a woman chose the queen of swords to represent herself. One of the possible meanings of the card is widowhood, so when it showed up in the first house of self in a horoscope spread, we suspected she was recently widowed. She confirmed that her husband had died less than a year before.

The king of pentacles appeared in the partnership position. Since it clearly wasn't her dead husband and she hadn't assigned court cards to anyone else in her life, we drew a second card for additional information. The six of cups turned up, a sure indication that someone from her past, perhaps a childhood friend she hadn't seen in years, was about to resurface in her life. She claimed the man had already appeared; they had dated thirty years ago, before she had met the man she married.

KNIGHTS AND PAGES

These two court cards often infuriate neophytes and pros alike simply because their meanings are so diverse. Knights can represent people of either gender between the ages of twenty-five and forty, thoughts, situations, or movement. Sometimes they symbolize all four. Pages can represent messages or young people. Knights are rarely used as significators, but pages may be used to denote a child. In a given reading, however, how do you know which of the possible definitions the particular card represents?

Our advice is to take a look at the surrounding cards. If the page of cups (birth, rebirth, renewal) shows up next to the

Empress (motherhood, fertility, pregnancy) and the reading is for a woman, then there's a very good chance that she or someone close to her is pregnant. If this combination shows up in a reading for a man, his wife or significant other may be pregnant or he is in a period of increase—new projects, new ideas, new job.

If the page of wands shows up in a spread about jobs and employment, then good news about a promotion, a raise, or a new job is on the way. A page of coins might indicate that good news about money is imminent.

Pages possess a marvelous quality of wonder about them. They often symbolize an enthusiastic student whose course of learning would depend on the suit. A page of coins might be a business student; a page of cups might be a student of the occult. Again, note the surrounding cards or draw additional cards for more information.

If the page and eight of pentacles appear together, then the chances are quite good that the querent is or will be in school. The new skills result in a small increase in income.

Knights often show up in readings when a person's life is in a state of flux, change, transition. They usually indicate situations, but can also represent people who are moving into or out of our lives. They can indicate physical travel and may precede a period in life when some long-standing situation suddenly begins to change.

The meanings assigned to pages and knights vary widely. Eileen Connely considers the knights emotional energies that explain a reaction to the seed planted by the page. Mary Greer says, "Knights act on, are involved in, and committed to the things indicated by their suit. They represent pure energy and often show where you are putting your energies. . . . For women, knights often represent an animus figure, especially a romantic one."

Sandor Konraad pegs knights as thoughts; the type of thought is defined by the suit. One reader we know sometimes interprets knights as the animals in our lives: domestic pets, wildlife we see frequently, animals that fascinate us. You probably won't find that interpretation in a book, but the point is that it works for the reader.

Regardless of which expert you read, his or her definitions may not necessarily work for you. As always, the best definition for any card in tarot is the one you learn through trial and error.

Kings

Kings represent closure, completion, the apex of an experience or situation, finality. They are about releasing old patterns of behavior so that you can move on with the rest of your life.

As people, kings are mature men who have achieved a measure of wisdom about who they are and what they can accomplish. They can also represent these attributes in women. A king is a father, uncle, older brother, or an older friend in whom you confide.

KING OF WANDS

He's an entrepreneur with considerable vision who takes risks to achieve his goals, a self-starter with limitless enthusiasm and energy. He may be self-employed, working independently in promotion, public relations, advertising, sales, or business.

This king sometimes has a temper that flares when he doesn't get his way. However, he can be an inspiration to others because his mere presence is a motivation to them to live to their greatest potential. He's linked astrologically with the element of fire: Aries, Leo, or Sagittarius.

IN A READING: An older man in your life inspires you. He pushes you to excel, to use your full potential. He encourages and supports your dream, whatever it may be. His relentless drive and energy sometimes irritate the people closest to him, but no one disputes the fact that he gets things done.

WORK: Innovative ideas besiege you. A boss or coworker proves instrumental in your implementation of new methods. Your business prospects improve, orders increase, your self-reliance is infectious. Curb your impatience, don't browbeat others into seeing things your way. Success is within your grasp.

ROMANCE: You're so caught up in your business and career concerns, you can't be bothered right now with passion and seduction. Be sure, however, that you don't cut yourself off emotionally from the people who are closest to you. Combined with the eight of cups, you walk way from a current relationship.

FINANCES: Innovation and originality lead to improvement in your financial situation. Orders increase. You're hooked into the prosperity loop. By pursuing your hunches, you discover you have a talent for entrepreneurial projects. Paired with the nine of pentacles, financial security is closer than you believe.

HEALTH: Migraines, heartburn, or problems with your sciatic nerve are improved through alternative therapies: acupuncture, diet, vitamins, minerals, and herbs. Experiment until you find what works best for you. Anger affects your health, so pinpoint what angers you and take steps to rectify it. Your overall health improves when you find a more moderate pace.

SPIRITUALITY: Your journey is underway. Remain open to possibilities and opportunities that seem to come to you out of nowhere. Follow impulses and pay attention to synchronicities; they are the signposts in your journey.

EMPOWERMENT: Your self-reliance and confidence propel you forward.

KING OF CUPS

He's a metaphysician or a preacher, a cook or the owner of a restaurant, a counselor or psychologist. His profession, whatever it is, reflects his compassion and the nurturing aspects of his personality.

His home and family are important to him and he may operate a business out of his home. He seeks financial independence, but not profit for the sake of profit. He wants to work at something that he enjoys. His astrological element is water: Pisces, Cancer, or Scorpio.

IN A READING: This king is something of a romantic, the kind of man who sends flowers even when it's not your birthday. His emotions often seesaw between evasiveness and bluntness, but don't take it personally. He generally feels more comfortable listening to others than talking about himself. He tends to rely too much on his feelings and needs to scrutinize whatever he undertakes with the sharpness of his intellect.

WORK: You work or want to work out of your home and are taking steps to make this a reality. Profit isn't your sole motive; your work has to be something you love doing. Your heightened intuition leads you to new opportunities. Paired with the seven of wands, self-employment is your goal.

ROMANCE: You meet someone through metaphysical groups or activities related to boating, sailing, or swimming. Your overall mood is flirtatious, adventurous, and intuitive. If you're already involved in a relationship, you and your significant other reach a new level of understanding. Perhaps you even renew old vows. Paired with the four of wands, marriage or a move are among the possible options.

FINANCES: Your home business flourishes, your orders increase, the money starts rolling in. You can't wait to leap out of bed in the morning to start your day. By fostering the belief that money is simply energy that you can manifest, you draw prosperity and opportunities for financial success.

HEALTH: You benefit from massage, energy work, foot reflexology. Curb your appetite, don't overindulge in alcohol. Take up swimming or sailing as a way to work off stress. You need periodic breaks—a trip to the beach, a week by a lake, any kind of relaxing travel that involves water. Don't fight against your fluctuating moods; ride with them.

SPIRITUALITY: Your answers are close to home, maybe as near as your bookshelf. Augment your intuitive experiences with metaphysical books on topics that pertain to your situation. Your deepest inspirations come through dreams, so keep a dream journal. By consciously requesting dreams that answer your questions, you harvest the richness of your own being.

EMPOWERMENT: You get in touch with your feelings so your intuition has room to flow.

KING OF PENTACLES

As the embodiment of worldly success and accomplishment, this king is the proverbial "square peg in a square hole." He is king of all he surveys and may be a wealthy businessman, financier, CEO, manager, industrialist, banker, media mogul, or successful artist. He is often self-employed.

Above all, he is secure within himself and in his position in society. He sets achievable goals, takes measured risks, and builds from each accomplishment. In his practical, no-nonsense way he keeps extending himself, slowly but steadily pushing upward. He's an earth sign: Capricorn, Virgo, or Taurus.

IN A READING: A business or professional contact helps with practical matters. This man is pragmatic, responsible, trustworthy, and always concerned with quality. Some may perceive him as dull. However, no other type has his confidence or ability to plan and produce.

For a woman, this king often means that a man with these qualities is close to her or will soon enter her life. For a man, this king usually indicates help from a father, older brother, or a boss.

WORK: You gain through professional contacts. Unexpected validation comes from an influential or powerful person. Projects that you've been working on are now nearing completion and you're gearing up for the next major undertaking.

ROMANCE: Whether you're uninvolved or committed, a courtship ensues in which you're wined, dined, and treated like royalty. Passions are unleashed, a past-life connection is made, a deep level of understanding is achieved. Travel with your significant other is indicated; expect romantic weekends in far-flung spots. If it is placed next to the Lovers or the three of cups, marriage may be in the offing.

FINANCES: Prosperity is here, now. The challenge lies in making newer and better deals. Guard against materialism as the only goal and don't get bogged down in nitpicky details. Maintain balance and approach the prosperity with a sense of fun and playfulness.

HEALTH: Tension may show up in your neck and shoulders, your stomach, and your knees. If you're a runner, try something else for a while that doesn't exert so much strain on your knees. Change your diet, allow for diversity. Any medical tests you undergo come back negative. Your biggest enemy is internalizing sorrow, emotional pain, or anger; these emotions take up residence in your body and may turn to illness.

SPIRITUALITY: You're feeling restless without quite knowing why. Evaluate what you need to feel emotionally fulfilled and go after it with the same relentless energy that has propelled you to material prosperity.

EMPOWERMENT: Build on past achievements to pursue new goals and dreams.

KING OF SWORDS

This warrior/scholar/diplomat may be a policeman, lawyer, judge, doctor, writer, philosopher, general, or president. He represents law and order and the justice of the establishment. He cuts ruthlessly through what he perceives as unnecessary or illogical. He often has the last word in matters of life and death.

Due to his association with authority, this king can symbolize the head of a company or a department. He provides wise counsel and although he rarely vacillates on important issues, he weighs everything carefully. The astrological element of this king is air: Gemini, Libra, or Aquarius.

IN A READING: You're put on notice that it may be time to cut away from old ideas and beliefs that have outlived their purpose. However, be fair and logical when making decisions that affect other people. There may be dealings with lawyers, physicians, judges, or the legal system in general. You may rely too much on your intellect; learn to listen to your intuition.

WORK: Your boss or a male coworker doesn't mince words and seems oblivious to how his opinions affect you. His judgments are swift, stripped to the bone, but fair. You admire his mental agility and ideas and this is the level where you communicate most effectively. When combined with the Tower, you may be fired or laid off from your job.

ROMANCE: Your significant other is blunt, sometimes to the point of indifference. Don't react emotionally; give yourself some breathing space, then calmly explain why you object to the bluntness. Your link with your significant other is primarily mental. With the Lovers, you're facing a choice about the relationship. With a knight or the Chariot, the relationship benefits by the two of you getting away for a short vacation.

FINANCES: The tension you've been experiencing about money matters comes to a head. Deal with it in a straightforward manner, then go on and don't look back. This dissolves the block and allows the "prosperity flow" to move into your life again.

HEALTH: A visit to your doctor results in a battery of medical tests. If surgery is recommended, get a second opinion, do

your own research. Then work with your doctor in an edu-
cated manner to come up with the treatment that best suits
your needs and what you can live with. With the Sun or the
Star, the doctor's visits and medical tests prove to be in your
favor. If you're pregnant and this card shows up with the
Empress or the ace of cups, a Cesarean may be a possibility.

SPIRITUALITY: Your spiritual path begins on a mental level,
through an intellectual curiosity about religion, philosophy,
metaphysics. Read, study, research. Once you've found your
intellectual niche, you become immersed emotionally in
your path.

EMPOWERMENT: Your sharp intellect cuts to the heart of any
matter.

Queens

They represent female energy, the yin, the receptive qualities
of the inner self, and the female influence in society. They
often appear as you approach the completion of a relationship, a project, a job, a pregnancy.

As people, queens are mature women who have confronted
the duality in themselves, incorporated it into who and what
they are, and now enjoy the wisdom their knowledge has
brought them. They represent mothers, wives, mistresses or
lovers, sisters; bosses and coworkers; friends.

QUEEN OF WANDS

She is businesslike and exuberant about everything she does.
She seems to have inexhaustible reserves of energy, has a flair
for drama, and is passionate about things she believes in.

Her temperamental behavior infuriates even the people who are closest to her, but it's simply part of who she is. Accept it because she isn't going to change. She's all fire: Aries, Leo, Sagittarius.

IN A READING: Your life right now focuses on work and/or your spiritual beliefs. You're filled with new ideas that you're anxious to implement in your profession or in spiritual work. An older woman proves helpful—or she interferes; look to the surrounding cards.

WORK: Expect an improvement in work and good news about your employment in general. Your female boss is firmly in your court. For a man, this queen means you may become involved with an older woman at work and the affair will be passionate and fulfilling. News is on the way about an issue or situation that has concerned you.

ROMANCE: You're swept up in a sudden affair marked by passion and intense emotions. Expect the unexpected; this person is impossible to pigeonhole. As a result, you enter into unknown terrain. At the heart of the affair lies a profound spiritual connection. Travel may be involved in this relationship and any trip to a foreign place will highlight flaws and strengths in the relationship. For a married man, this queen may represent his wife or the other woman in his life.

FINANCES: You splurge on a shopping spree, love every minute of it, then feel guilty afterward. Overall, your finances are volatile. Sell stocks that fluctuate wildly and buy land. Spend money on your home, refurbishing, remodeling, whatever it takes to get it ready to sell. You won't be staying where you are for long.

HEALTH: Your health is robust, although you may want to lose a few pounds. You experiment with homeopathy, herbs, vitamins, and take your body's cues. Guard against frayed nerves. Herbs may prove beneficial: green teas for the immune system, melatonin for a good night's sleep, ginseng for energy and estrogen production.

SPIRITUALITY: You seize your path and rush enthusiastically forward, devouring details, sampling everything. Remember to slow down and enjoy the journey. Follow your hunches about the direction you should take.

EMPOWERMENT: You possess the energy and enthusiasm to create the life you desire.

QUEEN OF CUPS

She's the prototypical nurturer, her heart filled with compassion. Her nurturing extends to children, animals, environmental issues, and causes in which she fervently believes. She excels in metaphysics and may be a clairvoyant, a psychic, a tarot-card reader, an astrologer. She can also be involved in undercover work, acting, or in medicine.

This queen's nature is spiritual and loving, but also sexual and often secretive. If you cross her, you'll pay the price. Her element is water: Pisces, Cancer, or Scorpio.

IN A READING: Your world centers around children, animals, metaphysics, nature, sex, and not necessarily in that order. You're unpretentious and comfortable with yourself. For a man, this queen may represent his mother, wife, or significant other, or the intuitive qualities he seeks to develop in himself.

WORK: A new opportunity comes your way and it hits you just right. This is work that satisfies or fulfills you emotionally.

Your female boss takes you under her wing or your own mother proves instrumental professionally. You're happiest when working from your own home, surrounded by your pets and the accouterments of your world.

ROMANCE: Sexual electricity seizes you; the affair is passionate, tumultuous, and incredibly romantic. Dreams become a vital source of information about the relationship, perhaps pinpointing past-life connections. You may have visions or clairaudient experiences about the relationship. Maintain your equilibrium and normal routines so that the passion of the liaison doesn't swallow you whole.

FINANCES: When you're not blocked emotionally, prosperity rushes into your life. Take advantage of it, play your hunches. You're lucky at the track, lucky in Las Vegas, lucky in finding deals. You've got your eye on a piece of property that may be on or very close to water; go ahead and buy it.

HEALTH: Your emotions have a powerful impact on your health. If you're blocked emotionally, it manifests somewhere in your body. Possible trouble spots: feet, lymph system, reproductive system, digestion. You benefit from regular exercise, massage, acupuncture, aerobics, and moderation in your diet. If you're stressed out and this queen appears next to the six of cups, children are the source of the stress. Paired with the ace of cups or the Empress, you may be pregnant.

SPIRITUALITY: Your spiritual path flows through all areas of your life. Your dreams are particularly vivid and you benefit from the study and practice of lucid dreaming. Your exploration of nonordinary realms is enhanced through group participation in shamanistic rituals, meditation, healing, and working with animals and children.

EMPOWERMENT: Time spent with loved ones, however brief, recharges your energy and propels you full speed ahead.

QUEEN OF PENTACLES

She is the Empress in her guise as Mother Earth and represents the procreative, nurturing, and protective aspects of motherhood. She showers her creations with lots of TLC and it doesn't matter whether they are actual children or projects and activities.

This queen rules her home and office with equal efficiency. She's infinitely practical, a go-getter, and may be an artist, writer, actress, dancer, or business executive. Her astrological element is earth: Capricorn, Taurus, Virgo.

IN A READING: You're seeking practical, tangible solutions. You come up with a business plan, a strategy, or a publicity campaign that your coworkers or employees can implement effectively. On the home front, your family is looking for the same kind of guidance from you. Paired with the Magician, your solutions come to you through flashes of inspiration.

WORK: Professionally, you build on your achievements and are recognized for them. You're not impulsive. You love what you do, but you're happiest within your personal space, surrounded by books, music, animals, plants, the private world you've created. Paired with the ten of pentacles, expect a dramatic increase in income.

ROMANCE: You're not in a big hurry to be involved right now. You've reached a place that suits you, even if it's solitary, and you are discovering it's okay to spend a Friday night at home with your pets and a good book. If someone interesting happens along, fine, but you're not out there looking. If you're committed, you and your significant other enter a peaceful, prosperous period in your relationship.

FINANCES: Your money situation is quite good, better than it's been in a while. Your Midas touch works so well you don't question it; you go with the flow. You enjoy the challenge of pitting your intellect against the odds. This is the time to buy property, stocks, a new home. Splurge. You deserve it.

HEALTH: Your overall health is good. It's the little things that bother you—a sore knee, tension in your neck, a tightness in your stomach when you feel anxious. Medical tests come out in your favor. If you're pregnant, the pregnancy will go smoothly. Make sure you and your doctor are clear about what you want during labor and delivery. Spell it out, be firm.

SPIRITUALITY: You enter a spiritually rich period of your life, in which your intuition and your reason work beautifully together. Everything seems to be clicking into place.

EMPOWERMENT: You use your wealth and abilities to empower yourself and others.

QUEEN OF SWORDS

This queen is Pallas Athena, the great warrior queen. She is something of a dichotomy, however, because her readiness to do battle is combined with femininity and creative intelligence.

A woman alone, this queen may be widowed or divorced and is sometimes childless. She is probably an independent career woman with her own ideas and values. Quite often, she is viewed as sister-consort, rather than wife, to the King of Swords. Astrologically, her element is air: Aquarius, Libra, Gemini.

IN A READING: You know how to cut through extraneous information to get to the heart of the matter. You tend to be outspoken, your tongue is sharp. Although you're usually fair and just, you can be vindictive. Secretive by nature, you're able to detect secrecy in others. Things don't come easily; you may have to defend your position and fight for what is rightfully yours.

WORK: Your boss or a coworker cuts you off. By remaining emotionally detached and conducting yourself in a courteous, efficient way, you overcome the slight and minimize professional injuries. Be discreet, keep your opinions to yourself.

ROMANCE: You're attracted to someone who is mentally quick and agile, but not very warm. A mother or an older woman may come between you and your significant other. She doesn't mean to interfere and she has your interests at heart, so be gentle but firm. Spell out your limits. If paired with the High Priestess in a man's reading, he's attracted to an older woman's mysterious lure.

FINANCES: Expect a delay. You may have to draw down your savings, sell some stock, or see an attorney. Rather than selling your home yourself, get a Realtor. Use professionals and don't try to do it all yourself. Put off buying small luxuries until your finances are more stable.

HEALTH: Surgery is a possibility. If paired with the three of swords, it may entail your heart. Look deeper than the physical. What situations or relationships are you clinging to that need to be released? Identifying and dealing with them may do you more good than the surgeon's knife.

SPIRITUALITY: Once you learn to incorporate your intellect and your emotions, your spiritual path becomes clear. You pursue your path alone.

EMPOWERMENT: Having overcome many difficulties, you face the future knowing who you are and where you are going.

Knights

They represent people or situations. The surrounding cards tell you which it is and which area of your life will be affected.

If a knight is an actual person, it indicates a young man or woman who enters your life. If the knight is a situation, it suggests that some long-standing condition in your life is changing, moving forward again. Travel is related to the knight's suit.

KNIGHT OF WANDS

Think of a young Indiana Jones, a traveler and adventurer for whom the quest is everything. His eagerness and energy burn at the center of his being and always propel him forward. He doesn't look back.

This knight possesses a deep spiritual center that even he may not be aware of consciously. The answers he seeks are to questions he hasn't asked yet, but in his relentless travels he somehow manages to find pieces of the larger puzzle and this keeps him moving. Synchronicity is at work in this knight's life; he appears at the right place at the right time.

IN A READING: You find what you're looking for before you even know you're looking. The bottom line is to get on with it, do whatever it is you've been wanting to do. Remain upbeat and positive; these attributes help your current situation change more quickly.

WORK: Travel is related to work and spiritual issues—a weekend of management training, for instance, or a workshop on past lives. Things at work are in flux, with employees being promoted and fired and new people being hired. You're not affected directly, except that the changes create commotion around you. Paired with the four of wands or the six of swords, your office moves to a new location.

ROMANCE: You meet someone through work, a spiritual group or activity, or while traveling. The attraction is immediate. If you're already involved, you and your significant other may work in the same office or operate a small business together. Although you have petty disagreements from time to time, you agree on the major issues. If you're not living together now, you may be soon.

FINANCES: You've been in a period where your financial growth was stymied or hovering at a particular plateau. With this card, everything moves forward. You have extra cash to pay off bills or put a down payment on a home.

HEALTH: Nagging health problems take a turn for the better. But you need to identify what kind of work you would like to be doing and then create a plan that will help you achieve your goal. Take stock of your beliefs. Discard the ones that no longer fit your experience.

SPIRITUALITY: You're on the move, actively searching for your particular spiritual path. The challenge lies in incorporating what you learn into all aspects of your life. You can no longer pigeonhole or hide your beliefs; it's time to step into who you really are.

EMPOWERMENT: Your fiery nature, confidence, and enthusiasm help you reach your goals.

KNIGHT OF CUPS

He is part Don Quixote, a troubadour who brings social activities, romance, excitement, and travel into your life. His charm is his greatest asset and his most powerful weapon. With it, he wins over his adversaries, converts people to his way of thinking, and moves through life with the grace of a fish.

This knight's focus is on emotion and on the creativity that flows from it. He is usually warmhearted and communicative, but sometimes he's so caught up in his own head he seems evasive, too self-contained. If you annoy him, he isn't the type who will tell you off; he'll simply tune you out.

IN A READING: A new kind of experience moves into your life. It buoys your spirits, stirs your compassion, and changes your beliefs about what is possible. This knight symbolizes the path with heart. Your tensions and loneliness ease as your emotions find an equilibrium that has been absent in recent months.

WORK: When you approach your responsibilities and projects in an intuitive way, your work conditions improve. You receive a prompt and probably emotional response to a professional issue you've tackled. Guard against excessive displays of emotion; it won't get you where you want to go any faster. Bide your time, success is a heartbeat away.

ROMANCE: You travel with your significant other and the trip brings you closer together. You're on the same wavelength. If you're not involved with anyone, a new affair begins that literally lights up your life. You experience sudden bursts of attention from the opposite sex, flirtations, romantic interludes. Coupled with the eight of pentacles, you'll meet someone new through classes or workshops.

FINANCES: Money seems to go out as fast as it comes in, and yet you experience increase and improvement. You feel lucky, however, and play the numbers that win in the lottery, at the track, at Las Vegas. You return home with more money than you had when you left. Now is the time to follow your parents' advice: Save ten or fifteen percent out of everything you earn.

HEALTH: A significant improvement is brought about, in part, by a new love affair. You benefit through foot reflexology, massage, any physical activity involving water, and through romantic sexual interludes. Ask for a healing dream; the results will astonish you.

SPIRITUALITY: By taking the path with heart, a new country of the spirit opens up. Your dreams provide direction and help answer your questions. Be alert for synchronicities and for a single day, attempt to interpret the experiences of your waking life as though they were part of a dream.

EMPOWERMENT: You delve into your deepest beliefs and emotions and reach an understanding about how they create what you experience.

KNIGHT OF PENTACLES

He is responsible, hardworking, doggedly serious, dependable and sometimes a bit dull. He works behind the scenes, planning and organizing everything for the other members of the court. He isn't afraid of hard work and is more concerned with the how than the why of life's duties.

His adventures focus on practical matters; this is the individual who may manage finances for a celebrity, for example. Expect travel related to money and business, media, advertising, and promotions. You may invest in real estate, buy or sell a home, buy or cash in a CD, or open new money-market accounts. The focus is on money and financial stability.

IN A READING: Set financial goals and stick to them. This can include putting together a budget, socking money away for your children's education, or saving the down payment for a home. Your finances improve steadily but surely. You find your niche—or it finds you.

WORK: You uncover a gold mine in a client or project and if you play your cards right, you're headed for professional success and distinction. Your new employee works relentlessly hard and is a credit to your company. Your focus now is on finding and nurturing projects that bring in a steady income and attract loyal customers.

ROMANCE: A hardworking, prosperous lover enters your life. Don't expect flowers or romantic dinners; you're more likely to get a weekend at the country manor or a cruise on the family yacht. Your significant other is attentive, but maybe not in the way you would like. Accept that you can't change this person and enjoy the relationship for what it is. You'll be happier that way.

FINANCES: A windfall. It comes through the stock market, a project, a winning lottery ticket, a large advance on a book. By doing your research and playing a hunch, you win big time. Don't squander it, but enjoy it. Travel related to money and finances is indicated.

HEALTH: Your general health is good, but you may be going through a few bumpy spots—an upset stomach, a tight neck, minor problems with your knees. If medical tests are ordered, they come back negative and you leave the doctor's office with lifestyle recommendations. Believe that you deserve excellent health, that you live in a state of health, and you will.

SPIRITUALITY: The big issues appear in your life all at once and trigger a search for answers. You don't merely react; you deal with the issues and evolve.

EMPOWERMENT: You willingly accept obligations and take responsibility for your own actions.

KNIGHT OF SWORDS

Like the young Alexander the Great, the Knight of Swords charges forward, conquering everything in his path. He rides bravely into the storm, waving his sword, all bravado and courage, eager to overcome every obstacle. This card addresses the need for both a mental and a physical show of strength. It represents a brave and aggressive young man who is prepared to defend his beliefs.

When this knight symbolizes a situation rather than an individual, expect a sudden whirlwind of social activity. This may include short trips out of town, gatherings where ideas are exchanged (conferences or workshops), and a sudden, positive surge in your work.

IN A READING: You're focused on making your point. Although you're a superb communicator, you usually act on your opinions rather than talking them to death. You can be headstrong and overly aggressive, given to speaking out too freely and telling people where to get off. It's time to stop talking about what you're going to do and just do it. Don't hesitate to express your opinion. You can win over any adversary with solid reasoning and logical arguments.

WORK: Go after your raise, your promotion, a project, book contract, movie deal, whatever it is that you want. You find allies in unexpected places. People around you admire your drive and ambition. Your traveling right now is related to the achievement of a specific goal. Don't let the pursuit of the goal overwhelm you, i.e., take time for the clichés, like pausing to smell the flowers.

ROMANCE: Whether you're involved in a relationship or not, you feel restless and unsettled, as though something is missing from your life. You want more than what you have, but then again, don't we all? Bide your time. Carve out space for yourself and your own interests and your significant other comes around.

FINANCES: Your efforts pay off in a big way. The long hours, the weekends and holidays you've worked, now begin to bear fruit. You enter a rewarding financial period in which your intellect is honed so sharply, you know almost instantly whether something will work or not. Don't be pushy; don't let your impatience deter you from your goal.

HEALTH: You seize control of your treatment or therapy. You apply your considerable skills to researching your health problem and arrive at the solution you believe is right for you. You no longer see yourself as a victim; this is the first step in your healing.

SPIRITUALITY: Your impatience works against you. Slow down, take time to process what's going on, listen to your heart, not your head.

EMPOWERMENT: Cultivate perfect faith that what you need will be provided before you need it. Be careful what you wish for.

Pages

When pages represent people, they are usually young children or adolescents. But quite often, a page may turn up for an adult who is emotionally immature.

Pages also represent messages or communication. They usually pertain to the beginning of whatever is represented by their suit.

PAGE OF WANDS

He is adventurous, spiritual, fun-loving, charismatic, and easily bored. This page has a tendency to begin projects he doesn't finish, to seek without quite understanding what he's looking for, and to think he knows more than he actually does.

He often represents creative seeds you have planted that are now beginning to sprout. The project you've been nursing for months is nearly ready to be presented; the novel you've been writing is almost finished; you're ready to enroll for a weekend workshop involving spiritual growth. His astrological element is fire: Aries, Leo, or Sagittarius.

IN A READING: You look for an agent for your novel or screenplay. You begin experimenting with out-of-body travel and other nonordinary realities. Regardless of your chronological age, you're touched by the wild spirit of youth. Don't abandon your goals; success lies within your grasp.

WORK: Expect messages concerning work or employment. If you've applied for a job, you hear that you got it. You initiate new projects or take over projects started by other people. This may entail a ghostwriting gig, an editing job, or some other freelance endeavor. Paired with the World, it may indicate a prize, award, or recognition for work you've done. New opportunities seem to appear out of the blue.

ROMANCE: A phone call or e-mail you've been hoping for arrives. A new relationship sails into your life and it's just the kind of partnership you've been hoping for—fun, exciting, fulfilling. You and your significant other share common interests in books and theater, spiritual topics, and may even work together.

FINANCES: Your financial outlook improves. Your application for a mortgage with a lower interest rate is approved, you receive a refund check you weren't expecting, a loan is repaid with interest, you get a break on your credit card debt. Financial rewards come your way for some project you've launched. Now is the time to start a prepaid college program for your child or children.

HEALTH: No two ways around it: You need to make some changes in your eating and lifestyle habits. Cut out the fatty foods, go on a diet you can live with, join an exercise class, take a meditation course. Combine the physical with the spiritual and pay attention to the seemingly random cues in your life; this leads to improved health.

SPIRITUALITY: Discover your bliss and pursue it. Free yourself of limitations and restrictions imposed on you by others. You're going through a season of rebirth. It's spring in your heart. Wake up and move out of the darkness and into the light.

EMPOWERMENT: Your point of power lies in the present.

PAGE OF CUPS

He's sensitive, emotional, loving, and often psychic. He works best behind the scenes and often finishes what other people start. His powerful imagination is one of his strongest assets and provides him with a deeply creative and spiritual bent. His astrological element is water: Pisces, Cancer, or Scorpio.

This page's focus is on expansion, new beginnings, creative and spiritual development. His voice is the intuitive whisper that nudges you in the right direction at the right time, that prompts you to pluck a certain book off a shelf that just happens to provide you with information you need.

IN A READING: Something new is born in your life. The book idea you've mulled over the last few months finally spills out of you and right into your computer. Your business expands, finances take an upward swing. A pregnancy or the birth of a child is a distinct possibility.

WORK: The professional doldrums you've experienced recently are swallowed by an emotional freshness that surges in your career. It sweeps you to the place you long to be. You suddenly find yourself in the right place at the right time. A message you've anticipated arrives and fills you with renewed hope.

ROMANCE: A new relationship or a message concerning an existing relationship puts you in the space where you want most to be. All things now seem possible. You and your significant other may decide to live together. If one or both of you have children, make them feel a part of the decision.

FINANCES: You get a break and it abrades your recent anxiety about money. Listen to your intuition about investments. Buy stock in new companies or in those that exhibit a social conscience. If you're looking for land or a home, don't buy impulsively. Check out the fine print.

HEALTH: Your emotions, positive or negative, show up almost immediately in your body. Most vulnerable are your feet, legs, and reproductive system. Instead of rushing off to the doctor for a quick fix, listen first to your body. What is it trying to tell you? Coupled with the Empress, you're pregnant. Paired with the eight of swords, your labor may be long. With the four of swords, an abortion or miscarriage is possible.

SPIRITUALITY: Don't lose sight of your emotional enthusiasm. Study the esoteric sciences that seize your interest, and cultivate an inner stillness.

EMPOWERMENT: Once you seek your true path, you open yourself to all possibilities.

PAGE OF PENTACLES

He is the student/apprentice of the tarot. He signifies the type of enthusiasm and wonder that young children bring to new projects. Totally fascinated with his studies, he makes little distinction between work and play. Think of him as the equivalent of the computer nerd who is completely immersed in his virtual world.

Like the Fool, the page of pentacles is a perpetual beginner. There is a strong connection to the energy of the earth and to the solitary journey of the vision quest. Life is seen as a continual rite of initiation.

IN A READING: Practical idealism, finances, and education are primary in your life right now. Your enthusiasm infects others and carries you in to a state of mind where work and play become interchangeable. Expect messages regarding money, contract negotiations, all forms of financial wheeling and dealing.

WORK: You tie up a deal on property you lease for your new business. You receive good news concerning clients. Paired with the seven of wands, you sign a contract for a book proposal, a product you're promoting, or a home you've listed for sale. Any tests you've taken bring in high grades. Paired with the Magician, you may get hung up on computer gaming; so what, enjoy it.

ROMANCE: Your sense of responsibility about an existing relationship outweighs whatever emotional ambivalence you feel. You're compelled to see things through to wherever they're going to go, even if your heart isn't completely in it. A karmic connection between you and your significant other must be resolved before you can move on.

FINANCES: You're in a period now where your money sense is right on. Messages and communications about pending deals heighten your self-confidence. You *know* you're going to make that sale, clinch that deal, sell that property. You can't be deterred from your goals.

HEALTH: Any problems you have may be messages from your inner self trying to seize your attention. The most vulnerable areas of your body are your knees, digestive system, neck, and shoulders. What is making you uptight? What scares you so deeply you're hesitant to move forward? Ask, the answers are there.

SPIRITUALITY: It won't be long before you're teaching others what you've learned. This is especially true when this card is paired with the Hermit.

EMPOWERMENT: You approach every activity with enthusiasm. The rewards interest you less than the work itself.

PAGE OF SWORDS

He's a complete dichotomy. He relates to crusading, assertiveness, and outspoken communication but also indicates a tendency not to take problems seriously. He finds it easier to detach from problems than to solve them. He maintains the posture of watcher and ironic observer, which can sometimes denigrate into spying on other people. He's all air: Gemini, Libra, or Aquarius.

Like the queen of swords, the androgynous page is linked to Pallas Athena, the warrior goddess of ancient Greece. The connection to Athena emphasizes that swords represent intellect and that the page symbolizes the active, curious mind. As a significator, choose this card for a swarthy, young child of either gender.

IN A READING: It may be that the people you're involved with don't take you seriously. A heart-to-heart talk will help clear the air, but be prepared for some constructive criticism. Expect news concerning legal affairs—a summons or a contract. You study topics that fire your intellect.

WORK: You lock horns with a coworker who thinks he's your intellectual superior. Don't lose your temper, don't preach your point of view. The matter can be resolved by exploring his side of the argument without losing sight of or compromising your principles. You receive a contract you've been waiting for. Let your attorney look it over before you sign.

ROMANCE: You and your significant other disagree on several major points in your relationship. You each try to change the other's mind about the issues, an exercise in futility. Just back off, give yourself some space, and the whole thing blows over. Significant developments then unfold; paired with the two of cups, one of those developments could be marriage.

FINANCES: Your financial acumen is considerable, but sometimes naive. Seek out the experts—a real-estate broker to sell your property, an attorney to peruse your contracts, a stockbroker to advise you on stock purchases and sales. Learn to delegate. You can't do it all by yourself.

HEALTH: You're burned out by long hours, too much work, and no play. Take a long weekend and do what you love best. You'll return with a fresh perspective and renewed energy. Nagging health problems demand research, so throw yourself into it and come up with a lifestyle plan that suits you. Paired with the three of swords, surgery may be indicated.

SPIRITUALITY: Admit it: You need to attend to the larger issues in your life. Set realistic goals for your spiritual development, take classes, join a church or religious group, enroll in workshops, treat yourself to a psychic reading. Do whatever it takes to get on track.

EMPOWERMENT: You're a powerful thinker with a curious mind and keen insight into the human condition.

5

The Minor Arcana

You're in a foreign city. Your passport and your money have been stolen, you don't speak the language, and you don't have a clue where the American embassy is. In terms of the tarot, this situation falls under the energy of a major, the Tower.

As you're wandering around, trying to read a map that might as well be written in hieroglyphics, you bump into a guy you worked with eight years ago in Denver. He not only speaks the language, he's been living in this city for the last two years. And even better, he's got a buddy at the embassy who expedites everything for you.

Within a few hours, you have a replacement passport, money, and your friend has offered you free accommodations. In terms of the tarot, this turn of events would fall under the energy of minor arcana cards, the six of cups and perhaps the ace of pentacles.

This vignette illustrates how the energy of the major arcana cards is manifested through the minors. Even though your trip was thrown into utter chaos by the theft (the Tower), it was ultimately resolved in a positive way because you reconnected with your friend, who helped you procure a new passport faster than you would have on your own, and you ended up with a free place to stay.

Getting to Know the Minors

The minors are divided into four suits, each with ten numbered pip cards, just like a regular deck of playing cards. Even though there are more of these cards (forty) than of the majors or court cards, the pips are easier to learn because you can group them by numbers or by suits. Keep charts one and two handy while you're learning the meanings.

Once you know what each card means, you have to be able to integrate the definitions to weave a story, just as you do with the majors. This takes practice, but it's actually easier than it may seem at first.

Relative Importance of the Minor Arcana

We consider the twenty-two cards of the major arcana to be the most powerful in the deck because they concern major issues in our lives. The pip cards, however, are important precisely because they pertain to events that are important on a daily basis.

Most questions directed to a tarot reader don't relate to long-term goals or archetypal situations; they are about the here and now in terms of work and career, romance, finances, health, family, and spiritual matters.

When interpreting the cards in a spread, we suggest that you give equal weight to the majors, the court cards, and the minors, except when you're doing a reading that relates directly to life's larger issues. Sometimes you may choose to read with only the major or minor arcana in order to zoom in on a specific type of question.

Numbers and the Tarot

Pythagoras contended that the world is built upon the power of numbers. He believed that everything in life could be expressed through combinations of primary numbers. An understanding of the basic symbolism of numbers is especially helpful when studying tarot.

With the exception of the court cards, every card in tarot is linked with a number. The numbered cards of the minor arcana represent events in our lives at their different stages of development. One easy way to learn the pip cards is to study the meanings of the numbers ace through ten and combine them with the meanings of the suits. In chart two, we have defined the numbers and what they mean in a reading.

Personal-loss Cards

No single card in the tarot portends death. Even if there were such a card, it would be simply one possibility among many. The future is constantly shifting, in flux. Nothing is written in stone.

Among the minors are cards that can indicate personal loss

if surrounding cards support it. The type of loss is usually spelled out in the other cards and the intensity depends on what the person values most highly. To an elderly widow, the loss of a pet may be as devastating as the loss of a job or child support would be to a single mother of four.

Both the five and the eight of cups are about personal loss. In the first, the loss has plunged the individual into such depths of grief he can't see that something remains in his life. In the second, the individual has made a conscious decision to walk away from a situation or a relationship that no longer works. The five of cups suggests that an external event has brought about the grief; the eight of cups indicates that the loss was brought about by an internal event.

The seven, eight, and ten of swords represent different degrees of loss. With the seven, petty theft may be involved. It doesn't necessarily have to be a material possession. Quite often, the seven of swords means that you feel your emotions are being plundered or that you're being taken advantage of.

The eight of swords, by contrast, symbolizes the loss of a rational perspective. The individual feels confused, mentally trapped, as if there is no way out.

The ten of swords concerns the end of something: a relationship, a marriage, a job, a friendship. It often happens when a confidence is violated or a trust is betrayed, when a person feels he has been stabbed in the back.

The five of pentacles can indicate a loss concerning money or a job. The three of swords suggests emotional or mental anguish, the kind that often results from the end of a relationship. Even though the five of swords is about a gloating victory, it can make you feel as if you've actually lost something, perhaps because you've somehow betrayed the better parts of yourself in your struggle to win.

The telling with these "loss" cards lies in the combinations. For example, if the five of cups appears with the two of cups and the Tower, then a relationship probably ends abruptly and unexpectedly and results in anguish. If the five of cups shows up with the ace and four of wands, it suggests the loss of a raise or a promotion or even of a new job. It results in a possible move and eventual greater happiness for the person.

Whenever one of these troublesome minors appears, look to the surrounding cards for additional information and keep your interpretation simple. If the person you're reading for has questions or wants clarification on a particular point, then draw new cards.

Even if a reading consists only of negative cards, end on an upbeat note. Emphasize that free will is paramount. Never predict a death.

A Useful Tale

In the summer of 1996, Hurricane Eduord roared across the Caribbean and evolved into a category-four hurricane, with sustained winds of 145 miles an hour.

To residents of south Florida, this held terrifying reminders of Hurricane Andrew, which slammed into the Miami area four years earlier, packing winds that gusted to 160 miles an hour. Andrew devastated entire neighborhoods, flattened Homestead Air Force Base, and altered many lives forever. He remained a landmark in people's mind, a gauge by which we measured other storms.

Eduord, on the satellite photos, looked like the same kind of storm—a sentient being racing toward land. It was well developed, with a clearly defined and rather large eye, and although he was relatively small in terms of the area he covered, he packed devastating power.

The experts couldn't decide where he would make landfall. He moved on a north by northwest path and until he turned definitively in one direction or another, south Florida remained one of the possible targets.

We decided to do a reading on whether Eduord would hit our area. This wasn't by any means a frivolous question. We needed to know whether to take precautions: stock up on food and water, fill our cars with gas, put up storm shutters, or head for higher ground.

We selected three cards, all related to the storm's *immediate future*: the Tower, eight of cups, ace of cups.

Our interpretation was that people wouldn't take chances (the Tower). They would rush out to buy plywood and provisions, and put up hurricane shutters. The grocery stores would overstock on water, canned goods, and survival supplies. A hurricane watch would go up somewhere along the south Florida coast.

The storm, however, would turn its back on south Florida (eight of cups) by taking a northerly direction very soon, probably within a day (ace of cups). This reading also coincided with what we felt intuitively.

During the twenty-four-hour period that the National Hurricane Center waited for Eduord to make up his mind, the local grocery stores went nuts. Crates of water crowded the aisles (59 cents a gallon, three dollars and change for a crate of six); disposable barbecue grills were a bargain at $2.50 apiece; and canned goods proliferated like rabbits.

Neighbors speculated about where in south Florida it would hit, hurricane shutters went up, plywood sold out. Once we pulled our cards, we did nothing. According to society's present belief system, this is *not* normal behavior.

You can't rely on cards for something like this, not even if the reading is backed up by your intuition. Or so the paradigm says.

The next morning, a hurricane watch went up along a portion of the south Florida coast, from the Sebastian Inlet northward to South Carolina. About twelve hours later, the watch was removed from Florida and extended from the south Georgia coast to North Carolina, then from North Carolina to Long Island. Eduord began to dissipate as he traveled over cooler waters. Long Island got rain, but that was about it. Eduord amounted to lots of bluster and not much else.

The reading proved to be correct. But more than that, it lined up with our intuitive sense about the storm's direction, which is the most important point about any divination system. If the cards tell you one thing and your intuition tells you something else, go with your gut. But make sure it's intuition speaking, and not panic or fear or some other emotion that's colored by left-brain consensus reality.

CHART 1: SUITS IN TAROT

Wands: Work and spiritual issues, ideas, growth

> *Element:* fire

> *Season:* spring

Cups: Emotions, desire, the inner self

> *Element:* water

> *Season:* summer

Pentacles: Money, manifestation, prosperity, health, property

> *Element:* earth

> *Season:* autumn

Swords: The intellect, left-brain thinking, action

Element: air

Season: winter

CHART 2: NUMBERS OF THE MINOR ARCANA

Ace: Beginnings, new ideas, creative power, potential, first causes, primary impulses, promise. **In a reading:** Potential. A situation is about to begin or is already in its early stages. One is the number equated with the Source, the beginning and end of all things.

Two: Partnerships, relationships, polarities, balancing and/or coming together of opposite forces, duality, choices, decisions, a period of waiting, a respite. **In a reading:** This is a time of decision or choice, of finding the balance in duality and in partnerships.

Three: Synthesis, growth, creativity, abundance, collaboration, friendship, artistic expression, refining plans, preparing to take action. **In a reading:** Unity and group activities are emphasized. Refine plans set into motion at the one and two levels. Initial achievement of your goals.

Four: Foundations, discipline, work, order, stability, solidity, tangible achievement, practical attainment. **In a reading:** Things previously imagined and planned for at the three level begin to manifest. Your foundations are stable and solid.

Five: New cycle, change, progress, shifts, adjustment, fine tuning, instability, challenge, versatility, freedom, courage. **In a reading:** A need for change is indicated. Adjust and fine-tune all that has manifested at the four level. Expect uncertainty but know that it, too, shall pass.

Six: Balance, health, harmony in the face of change, contentment, relaxation, satisfaction, equilibrium. **In a reading:** Triumph over challenges addressed at the five level. Harmony and balance are indicated. Take heart: You're closer to your goal than you think.

Seven: Spirituality, wisdom, perfect order, the macrocosm, religion, luck, magic, multiple options. **In a reading:** You triumph over mundane problems at the six level and numerous options open up to you. A cycle has been completed.

Eight: Regeneration, rebirth, reevaluating, putting things in order, setting priorities. **In a reading:** You're sorting through the options experienced at the seven level in order to decide what to keep and what to release. Think regeneration, renewal.

Nine: Bringing things to a conclusion, integration, movement, flexibility, fulfillment, attainment. **In a reading:** Fulfillment; you complete situations that were met at the eight level and integrate them into your life.

Ten: Transition, renewal to a new cycle, completion, wholeness, mastery, excess, overabundance. **In a reading:** Transition to something new. An ending. Preparation for a new beginning.

Wands

Issues: Work, creativity, spiritual matters, growth, expansion, developing ideas, enterprise, energy, initiative, renewal

Astrological element: fire

Season: spring

ACE OF WANDS

This card signals a creative beginning, the birth of an idea, a raise or promotion or a new job, the start of a new enterprise, or new challenges. Associated with this ace are boundless energy, fiery enthusiasm, optimism, and exhilaration. It's a signal to proceed with whatever has sparked your interest and excitement.

IN A READING: Think *new*: a journey, a pregnancy, the birth of a child, a sexual escapade, or the opening of a business. Good news about work or spiritual matters arrives in the mail or by phone. A contract is signed, a manuscript sold, or an advance payment received.

Your head spins with new ideas. Now that you've laid to rest most of your doubts and hesitations, you're ready to quit your secure job and strike out on your own.

WORK: A new chapter begins. This may be a position that you've coveted, the sale of a book, the start of a new project, the opening of your own business. You find your niche, get a taste of all that might be and pursue your dream.

ROMANCE: A new relationship enters your life, the chemistry is immediate and powerful. You or your significant other undergo a spiritual renewal that pulls you closer together. Your passion in the relationship isn't focused just in the physical; there's a definite spiritual connection that lies, perhaps, in a past life.

FINANCES: Your earnings increase through a new opportunity that seems to sweep into your life from out of nowhere. Risks generate income. Your investments in environmentally aware businesses pay handsome dividends.

HEALTH: You begin a new treatment, consult a new doctor, or gravitate toward alternative therapies. A spiritual awakening affects your health in a positive way. Your improved physical condition becomes a springboard for psychic exploration. Pregnancy is a possibility.

SPIRITUALITY: A rebirth of the spirit takes place. You broaden your worldview and expand your idea of what's possible. The mind-body link is a reality for you. Seize the opportunity to follow your impulses. The results will astound you.

EMPOWERMENT: Your bliss grabs you and you go wherever it takes you.

TWO OF WANDS

Success is imminent. Your ships are coming in, although not as quickly as with the three of wands. You know what you're capable of, you understand what needs to be done. You also realize you're moving in the right direction and sense that your investment in ideas, time, and money are about to pay off.

IN A READING: You're involved in a working partnership and are pleased with the way things are unfolding. You and your partner think alike about the main issues and your goals mesh to form a seamless whole. Travel is either connected with work or with spiritual matters and you probably travel with someone else—a business associate or someone whose spiritual beliefs reflect your own.

WORK: You collaborate with another person on a creative or business project: a screenplay, a small business, a court case. You and your partner bring ideas together in new and unusual ways. You make the right connections, which benefit the partnership. Good news about cooperative efforts, work, and finances is on the way.

ROMANCE: You and your significant other concur on something you've both thought about for some time. The dream you share is your tightest bond, the glue that holds you together when the relationship is otherwise bumpy and uncertain. It may be a while before the dream becomes a reality, but the journey proves to be magnificent.

FINANCES: Yes, your raise is in the offing, the boss is happy about your work. But until the raise comes through, you're strapped for cash and the strain is starting to show. Resist the convenience of credit cards as long as you can. Trust that things are about to change. Your finances will improve significantly soon.

HEALTH: You're waiting for the results of medical tests. You feel confident that the tests will come back negative, but you suffer moments of doubt in which your worst nightmares unfold. Even if you can't make the leap of faith and sustain it, at least resolve to do something you enjoy. Break your routine. It will make the negative results of the tests that much sweeter.

SPIRITUALITY: You're planning to attend a spiritual retreat or workshop with a friend. The only thing holding you back is time. Forget the time. Do it now. You need the respite. Once you put out the word that you would like to attend the retreat, someone you know voices an interest in attending as well.

EMPOWERMENT: You hold the secret to your own growth. Open yourself to all possibilities.

THREE OF WANDS

You're poised on the threshold of success and your past efforts are starting to pay off. You've reached an important milestone; you are on solid ground and have developed a new confidence concerning your long-term plans. The focus is on commerce, overseas transactions, ventures involving imports and exports.

IN A READING: You've gone as far as you can by yourself; you need an infusion of group energy. The group doesn't have to be large—two or three others will suffice. But the others must be people with whom you can pool talents and ideas. From this supportive base you will move toward the future with renewed confidence.

WORK: Brace yourself: The change you've been waiting for is within sight. The enterprise that has consumed you and your partners is beginning to bear fruit—new orders arrive for your product or service; people who have heard about you through other satisfied customers come knocking at your door. You're promoted. Your book or screenplay sells, you have your first important art exhibit. In short, you're on your way.

ROMANCE: A soul mate appears in your life through a blind date or a casual meeting while you're out with friends. You share the same spiritual ideals and seem to mesh on every other level as well. A vacation with your significant other is indicated, someplace exotic and foreign that may involve travel by water.

FINANCES: Your business or student loan is approved. Your company turns a substantial profit and you and your partner reward yourselves with a trip. Make sure you sock some of the profits away or pour them back into the company. An expensive purchase is in the offing: a boat, a new car, a small plane.

HEALTH: The news is good. Your blood pressure is exactly where it should be for your age and body size, your choles-terol is fine, your pregnancy progresses well. You've finally figured out how to balance work and play. You sense a shift within yourself at the deepest levels and are hungry now for additional information on alternative therapies.

SPIRITUALITY: The many and varied ideas you investigate finally synthesize into a belief system, a way of looking at the universe and yourself. Now go out into the world and test its validity.

EMPOWERMENT: You possess the power to bring about your heart's desire.

FOUR OF WANDS

The keys are marriage or any committed relationship, busi-ness partnerships, friendships, great happiness in general. This four is associated with engagements, births, puberty, and the rites of passage from adolescence to adulthood. It can also mean a move—actual or metaphorical.

IN A READING: The purchase of land or a home is in the offing. You may make a physical move from one house, city, or state to another, perhaps because of a marriage. Your creative project moves from one company to another and flourishes.

Times are good; you feel safe and secure. Your plans are solidly laid, your foundations are firm. You've earned a time-out for rest and relaxation. Enjoy an outing, reunion, or holiday party with family and friends.

WORK: You get an offer from another company for more money and greater responsibility that you can't refuse. This is the door to your future; step through it with confidence. Your work involves a move to another city or state. Your office may move across town, to a better neighborhood. You enter a new and prosperous period in your profession.

ROMANCE: Your living arrangement takes a more serious, committed turn. You and your significant other decide to move in together or tie the knot. If you marry, the marriage is conventional, ritualized. If you're uncommitted, your work results in a move that proves beneficial and prosperous.

FINANCES: You change brokers, banks, mortgage holders, or all three. The sale of your creative project brings in big bucks. You're so busy making money you don't have time to spend it. The least you should do is open a Keogh, buy a CD, or invest in some land. Put your money to work for you on a long-term basis.

HEALTH: You change doctors or lifestyles and notice an immediate improvement in your health. You benefit from a temperate climate and the use of certain herbs and folk remedies. If you discover you're pregnant, you and your significant other will probably move when your child is born.

SPIRITUALITY: The foundations you've laid are so solid they see you through virtually everything. Your belief system may not be like everyone else's, but it serves you well.

EMPOWERMENT: Rejoice in your happiness. You've earned it.

FIVE OF WANDS

Others want what you want and the contest is likely to be exciting and heated, filled with action and rivalry. Don't allow your competitors to gain the advantage. Be firm, stand your ground, don't give in. Despite the uphill battle, you overcome the competition.

IN A READING: The competition refers to a business, social, or spiritual situation. You expend so much energy countering your rivals that it's interfering with the rest of your life, and you don't have time for your usual pursuits. So make time. Set aside space for yourself and your passions.

WORK: The competition for the job you want is stiff, frustrating. You're better off ignoring the gossip that proliferates in your work environment; just go about your business and do the best you can. Although you face a significant challenge, your efforts won't go unnoticed or unrewarded.

ROMANCE: You're competing with one or even several others who covet the same person who interests you. If you're committed, your significant other may be having an affair. You feel your work or that of your lover competes for the time you would rather spend with each other.

FINANCES: You're in the running for that raise or promotion you've been working toward, but it's an arduous battle. Right now cash is tight, your bills are squeezing you dry. You're robbing Peter to pay Paul. The secret is not to panic. Pay the minimum on your bills and trust that the squeeze is only temporary. If you have to, moonlight to ease the financial tension.

HEALTH: Your insurance company or your doctor or both are giving you the run-around. You're stressed out, your life seems to be moving too quickly, you need a break. The best course of action is to step back from the situation, appraise things honestly, and create a game plan. Then proceed with whatever it is you have to do.

SPIRITUALITY: Your normal routine competes with your spiritual time. Slow down, pace yourself, make the time for that workshop you want to attend or for a seminar or retreat that intrigues you.

EMPOWERMENT: You rise to the challenge.

SIX OF WANDS

Known as the victory card, this six relates to the successful completion of a task, project, or business venture. You have overcome all obstacles, triumph is nearly upon you. With a combination of persistence, intelligence, and clear vision, you achieve your cherished dream.

IN A READING: Welcome this card. It indicates that in spite of problems or delays you've experienced, you win. It portends vindication and reward for your hard work. Whatever it brings, you have earned it through drive, ambition, desire, and belief in your own abilities.

WORK: A new job, a promotion, a raise: Whatever it is you've been waiting for, the decision comes down and it's in your favor. You graduate with honors from school, you're recognized for the work you've done. Treat yourself to a weekend at a spa, a resort, or a camping trip under the stars. You've earned it.

ROMANCE: You win the man or woman of your dreams, it's as simple and as complex as that. If you're already committed, your significant other sees your side of things; a deeper understanding results. You now know when to keep your own counsel, when to speak up, when to back off.

FINANCES: Increase. Your stocks rise in value, you get your asking price for your home or property, you're paid a substantial bonus. That book you finally finished now sells for six figures or your horse wins big time at the track. You're in the money for sure.

HEALTH: As your career flourishes and your finances improve, your nagging physical complaints vanish as mysteriously and suddenly as they appeared. Your diet shows results, you quit smoking, your exercise program begins to pay off. You're in better shape now than you've ever been.

SPIRITUALITY: Your spiritual program, whatever it is, shows tangible results. During your daily meditation, you begin to receive the answers you need. Your attempts at lucid dreaming or out-of-body travel pay off. Your psychic abilities are accelerated. You radiate contentment and well-being.

EMPOWERMENT: Enjoy your triumph and realize that what you have manifested can be repeated again and again.

SEVEN OF WANDS

You possess the ability to succeed against all opposition. You're in an advantageous position. Face up to the situation, take a stand, don't hesitate to assert your own point of view. Because of its connection to wisdom and knowledge, this seven incorporates skills in teaching, lecturing, and composing. It's sometimes referred to as the writer's card, but encompasses all types of self-employment.

IN A READING: You're meeting the challenge, whatever form it takes. Your next step is to tie up the loose ends of the past and get on with your life. You triumph over the competition by making your own decisions and relying on your inner strength and judgment.

WORK: Your dream is to be self-employed and you've been working steadily toward its realization. This card puts you on notice that it's time to take the plunge. Forget the regular paycheck, the guaranteed benefits and perks; if you aren't happy doing what you're doing, then stop doing it. Believe in yourself and strike out on your own. You'll prevail no matter how hotly contested the market is or how clever the opposition seems to be.

ROMANCE: You feel stifled in your current relationship, stifled in your single status, stifled no matter which way you turn or who you meet. Even when you find someone you like, there are rivals for his or her affection. But it's just a phase. You come through it stronger than you were before, with a clearer idea of who you are and who you want to spend your life with.

FINANCES: Your small-business earnings start to increase, your manuscript sells, your risks begin to pay dividends. The battle seems all uphill at first, but by spring things turn around. Stay true to your vision.

HEALTH: Maintain your exercise program, your diet, whatever therapy you're using. Your body's innate wisdom rallies to your defense. You not only meet the challenge—you move beyond it. You benefit from martial-arts training, Tai Chi, and yoga.

SPIRITUALITY: Your beliefs are tested by someone whose convictions differ from yours or by someone who hopes to convert you to another way of thinking. Listen to what the individual has to say, weigh it against what feels right to you, then defend your position.

EMPOWERMENT: You stand up for your beliefs, meet your challenges and overcome the opposition.

EIGHT OF WANDS

This eight marks the end of a period of stagnation and delay. You're approaching your goal quickly, plans are nearing completion. Good news is headed your way and all forms of communication are highlighted, in particular faxes, e-mail, telephone calls. Travel is related to work, creativity, and spiritual pursuits.

IN A READING: Broaden your horizons, try out new ideas, begin new projects, and conduct your business in a newer, more innovative way. Use available technology to advertise your products or yourself—build a Web page, communicate via e-mail, learn to use your fax machine. The world is smaller than you think.

WORK: Advertising and promotion are favored, so are contracts that come by priority mail, fax, or e-mail. Travel is related to professional workshops, spiritual retreats, and anything that feeds your imagination and helps you reach your goals. Good news arrives, something that puts a different spin on the overall picture. Synchronicities proliferate in your life right now: heed them and try to understand the underlying message.

ROMANCE: You meet someone quickly, unexpectedly, and the two of you hit it off big time. You're attracted to the other person's spiritual beliefs or the work he or she does. If you're already involved, things heat up. One or both of you move; perhaps you move in together. Your open communication and complete honesty with each other enhance the relationship.

FINANCES: The check you've been waiting for arrives in the mail, a tip from your stockbroker pans out, your mortgage is approved rapidly, funds are transferred electronically. Financial progress is sudden and frequently unexpected.

HEALTH: Your healing speeds up, perhaps because of some belief shift you've made without consciously realizing it. Books about health and healing, as well as workshops on alternative therapies, stimulate your mind and spur your body's immune system. Things begin to click. You're on your way to wellness.

SPIRITUALITY: It all happens so fast. One moment you're a skeptic, the next moment you're immersed in a transpersonal experience that seems to slam into your life out of nowhere. It touches every facet of your existence.

EMPOWERMENT: Your quick response to information results in life-transforming experiences.

NINE OF WANDS

One last test or challenge remains. You feel as if you've come to the end of your fighting powers, but you have skill and determination in reserve. You're actually in a position of strength. Although you'll need to draw on all your courage and abilities, you prevail. Start planning your next course of action. Think before you leap.

IN A READING: Just when things seems to be clicking right along, you hit a glitch, a brief pause. It's a minor setback due to a miscommunication, but it bothers you nonetheless. One final interview stands between you and that job or club membership you covet. One more exam and you'll be accepted to the college of your choice, receive a clean bill of health, pass the bar, get your driver's license. Be patient, keep your own counsel. Once the last obstacle is overcome, you're home free.

WORK: Your book is optioned for TV or movies, your video grabs a producer's attention, your Web page is nominated for an award. In some way, your work is recognized and appreciated publicly and it comes at what appears to be an iffy time. You're called in for a final meeting about your new project, the bank needs more information before your loan is approved, the orchestra conductor asks you back for one more audition.

ROMANCE: A relationship has heated up to the point where one or both of you needs breathing space. You must decide whether you and your significant other envision a similar journey, similar goals. If you do, what are your expectations for the relationship? If not, can you live with it?

FINANCES: You've overdrawn your bank account, a check has bounced. Even though it's not your fault, it delays things. Your stock dips; you incur a large household expense—a refrigerator that goes on the fritz, a garage door that jumps its track, a heating or air-conditioning unit that needs to be repaired. You must dip into your rainy-day fund or increase your credit card debt.

HEALTH: An accretion of small irritations affects your immune system and results in a cold, a sore throat, laryngitis, fatigue. So take a day off, treat yourself to a day at the beach, a spa, a meditation workshop, whatever it takes to distract you. When you return, you'll feel better and have more energy.

SPIRITUALITY: You feel stagnated at the moment. Your spiritual searching seems to have hit an impasse. Stay resolved and disciplined, focus, concentrate, set a deadline. Do whatever it takes, but don't waver from your purpose. You're much closer to your goals than you think.

EMPOWERMENT: You've accumulated enough power, energy, and wisdom to overcome any obstacle.

TEN OF WANDS

This is the card of the workaholic—and of the individual on a mission. You've assumed so much responsibility you feel burdened. You probably don't want to delegate because you believe the old saw, "If you want something done right, do it yourself." You may resent the heavy load, but you enjoy playing martyr and missionary.

WORK: It's time to head out into the world and dispense your knowledge. You can certainly handle what you've taken on. But if it proves to be too much because of other commitments in your life, don't hesitate to release some of your responsibilities. Many of the burdens you carry are self-imposed. Make time to relax and enjoy life. You'll return to the fray refreshed and renewed.

ROMANCE: Whether you're single or involved, it's all become a burden. You're tired of the singles bar routine, tired of the dating routine, tired of the constant disagreements with your significant other. Step back, take stock, decide what you can live with and what you can't abide. Then move forward.

FINANCES: It's time to reevaluate your stock portfolio, your IRA, your pension plan, your investments. Your debt obligations oppress you. And yet you have the knowledge you need to get where you want to be; you simply haven't tapped it yet.

HEALTH: The therapies you try don't seem to work. You're tired of being overweight or stressed out or riddled with minor physical complaints. You benefit from time spent alone, from yoga, meditation, anything that forces you to concentrate on your breathing. Power walking may be the answer.

SPIRITUALITY: You feel compelled to finish an artistic endeavor that is also linked deeply to who you are—and who you're becoming. It creates a burden on your family and loved ones. Be honest about what you need; your loved ones will surprise you with their compassion and will give you the space you need.

EMPOWERMENT: You refuse to let your real or imagined responsibilities overshadow the joy of living.

Cups

Issues: emotions, relationships, romance, all affairs of the heart

Astrological element: water

Season: summer

ACE OF CUPS

If you're single and uncommitted a new love affair is on the way. If you're married or already involved, expect a passionate renewal of your relationship. Synonymous with the Holy Grail, this ace is a symbol of love that is intrinsically spiritual, which connects us to something larger than ourselves.

Think newness with this card—new love, new start, new appreciation for life, new fortune, new opportunities, joy, fertility, a spiritual awakening. A happy situation is about to start or is already in the beginning stages.

IN A READING: Your affair is no one-night stand; this is *love* in the purest sense of the word. Allow yourself to experience the joy of letting go into unconditional love and acceptance. Because of its connection to the archetypal feminine symbol of the vessel, this ace often relates to pregnancy and birth.

WORK: You embark on a new career or luck into a new job that fulfills you. If you're continuing in a long-term job situation that has become dull or sluggish, you discover innovative ways to approach your work and feel revitalized. You garner praise and admiration for your creative, inspired, and innovative ideas.

ROMANCE: Love at first sight quickly deepens into a serious romantic attachment. An engagement or wedding date is announced, vows are exchanged, a commitment is deepened significantly. Everything in the romance department clicks along far better than you ever expected.

FINANCES: Give serious attention to an unexpected opportunity to trade up to a new home, refinance your current one, or buy that long-desired big-ticket item at a steep discount. A new project spells a fortunate increase in your family's income. As a result, your financial base expands significantly.

HEALTH: Your health is fine. Your physical well-being improves in direct proportion to your mental outlook. If you're asking about a pregnancy and this ace shows up with the three, four, or five of swords, a miscarriage or Cesarean is possible.

SPIRITUALITY: Surrender, accept, permit! By remaining open to opportunity and embracing what comes your way, you embark on a journey into higher consciousness. This may entail workshops and retreats or studying with a mentor or spiritual teacher. Meditation opens your heart to the ecstasy of divine love.

EMPOWERMENT: In conflicts between heart and mind, you follow your heart.

TWO OF CUPS

Partnership of all kinds and marriage in particular are inherent to this card. In many ways it's more indicative of a love relationship than the Lovers. While the trump concerns commitment and choice in ongoing unions, the two of cups relates to romance, courtship, and passion that may ultimately lead to marriage.

Emotional balance and cordial personal encounters are hallmarks of this two. You accept with equanimity whatever life brings.

IN A READING: Friendship and companionship are highlighted. Get out of the house, enjoy yourself, spend time with people you care about. Dating and other social activities balance your life. Show your appreciation of your friends and family. It's a good time to settle minor disputes and resolve past differences. Before you can enter into a committed relationship with another person, you need to be clear within yourself about what you want and need in life.

WORK: Expect a smooth partnership that will benefit both parties. In your working environment, you encounter the harmony, pleasant surroundings, cooperation, and friendly atmosphere you desire. A contract is consummated. You get the job you applied for, are accepted to the college of your choice, win a raise or promotion or both.

ROMANCE: A strong sexual attraction resonates at deep, instinctive levels; a sense of déjà vu permeates your initial encounter. This two suggests the reunion of soul mates who seek to fulfill commitments begun in previous lives. You move in with your significant other; you decide to tie the knot.

FINANCES: Money comes through partnership and work that you enjoy. Group investments flourish. An unexpected stroke of good fortune allows you to clear up old debts and resolve long-term financial problems.

HEALTH: Significant improvement, perhaps even a remission, occurs with a serious condition. The emphasis is on keeping bodily functions on an even keel. Metabolism, heartbeat, blood pressure, and sugar levels should all be tested to make sure that everything is in perfect balance.

SPIRITUALITY: Your heart chakra opens, you feel at one with the universe. Your awareness of multidimensional reality is enhanced through out-of-body travel and lucid dreaming. You experience the harmony and connection of All That Is.

EMPOWERMENT: By uniting with another, you accomplish more than either of you could achieve alone.

THREE OF CUPS

Celebration. It may be the result of a marriage, the holidays, family reunions, births, baptisms, engagements, good fortune, success—in short, whatever fills you with joy.

The three of cups has a built-in timing element because of its association with holidays. For a question posed in the late summer and early autumn, expect something to happen between Thanksgiving and New Year's Eve. During the late summer and early spring, look to the Easter holidays. Any upcoming holiday or celebration can be used to fix the time of an expected event.

IN A READING: Your intuition blossoms, you clarify your emotions and belief system. If you've been reading cards or doing psychic readings just for friends, you'll soon "go public." If you've been mired in confusion about a relationship, the confusion will lift. A pending matter reaches a happy conclusion. Estrangements are mended in a joyful reunion. Old wounds heal and allow you to move forward in your life.

WORK: The office mood is festive, raises and bonuses are forthcoming. Everyone benefits from a large contract your company just won. Your accomplishments and contributions are recognized publicly. You use them as springboards to the next phase of your career.

ROMANCE: The joy of good times brings you together with those you love. Savor the happiness and fun of carefree social activity. If you're not involved, you meet the person of your dreams at a party, a gathering, or at someone else's wedding. If you're involved, you and your significant other may decide to exchange vows at a lavish gathering of friends and family. Yes, you probably overindulge. Instead of feeling guilty the next morning, enjoy the celebration.

FINANCES: It's easy come, easy go in financial matters. You get a raise, make a killing in the market, receive a generous inheritance. Then you turn around and pay it out for your daughter's wedding, your son's bar mitzvah, your second honeymoon, or a down payment on a vacation home.

HEALTH: You're happy with the results of a physical exam. Everything checks out great, but your doctor advises you to go on a diet, cut down on your indulgences, and take up an exercise program.

SPIRITUALITY: Group interactions with people of like mind lead to a spiritual awakening. Through shared ceremony and ritual you experience a renewed feeling of inner peace and reverence for the All.

EMPOWERMENT: You celebrate your life and share its joy and wonder with those around you.

FOUR OF CUPS

Suffused with apathy, you don't recognize new opportunity when it's presented. Take a second look; it may be better than you think. You have a lot going for you but are too full of discontent and self-pity to appreciate what you've got.

If you're experiencing occasional periods of mental and physical laziness, a fresh idea or interesting project will provide new momentum. This four is sometimes a wake-up call to recognize that your depression may be more than just a passing mood.

IN A READING: You have choices but consider them to be without merit. Even when someone offers you an opportunity, you greet it with disdain. Perhaps you're jaded by the good things in life; perhaps you're simply in a period where the future seems bleak. Whatever the cause, you're disregarding opportunities for growth, renewed happiness, and satisfaction.

WORK: Monotonous routine has drained you of your motivation. Stop spinning your wheels. Sulking and ill humor have no place in a professional setting. It's time to figure out what's bugging you and change it. If you hate your job, then look for something that suits you better. If you want a new career, then take steps to qualify yourself for it. Take action.

ROMANCE: Dissatisfaction, disillusion, or hurt feelings spell trouble in an ongoing relationship. Take time to focus specifically on what's bothering you and try to talk about it with your significant other. If there's no one special in your life right now, it's not because you lack for suitors. You're simply not interested in any of them. Remove your blinders.

FINANCES: You need a new source of income, but you keep overlooking the obvious. Reconsider opportunities or investments that you've flat-out rejected. Take another look at those rejection slips; did an editor who rejected your current manuscript leave the door open to your submission of another project? Things aren't as bleak as they appear to be.

HEALTH: Once you change your mental outlook, your health improves significantly. The source of your malaise stems from emotional or mental blocks or from a lack of understanding about your spiritual needs. A psychologist, minister, spiritual healer, or psychic can probably provide more help than a physician.

SPIRITUALITY: You're mired in a period of uncertainty. Perhaps your traditional religious beliefs no longer meet your needs. Nothing new that you've tried quite fills the void. Although you feel like a lost soul, you begin to unravel your confusion and gradually find the answers you seek.

EMPOWERMENT: Reevaluate your life and relationships with an eye toward uncovering possibilities that you may have overlooked.

FIVE OF CUPS

There's no way around it: This card is about disappointment, regret, and loss. It sometimes refers to an individual who has trouble releasing the past or has experienced an emotional loss that led to complete absorption in sorrow.

There may be an obsession over past wrongs. The bottom line is that it's time to pick up the pieces and go forward.

IN A READING: What's gone is gone. Concentrate on what you have left, not on what you've lost. Take time to experience your grief and disappointment, then move on. It's unwise to try to hide from your feelings, but is equally damaging to cling to unhappy memories. Examine your situation and see what you can learn from your distressing experiences. Then turn your back on the past and lay the foundation for your future.

WORK: Nothing is resolved or settled quickly. Expect delays and setbacks connected to job applications, interviews, test results, professional projects. On the job you feel tired and burned out. Indifference causes you to wonder about the road not taken. This card often appears when companies downsize or reorganize. If you're demoted or laid off, examine your real needs with brutal honesty. Is it possible that you were stifled in that job?

ROMANCE: The end of a relationship has left you feeling bereft, adrift, consumed with your loss. You want your former lover to return, but it's not going to happen. You and your depression keep each other company. Unable to face the emotional demands of a new relationship, you rebuff potential romantic partners.

FINANCES: You're being miserly in regard to money and or material goods. Financial loss plagues you and you're fed up with the accompanying problems, obstacles, and delays. Take a risk to get things moving again—look for another job, moonlight, strive to believe in yourself and your right to prosperity.

HEALTH: By harboring old grievances and dwelling on past disappointments, you make yourself ill. To improve physically, cut yourself loose from emotional sorrow. The cause of your dis-ease is essentially psychological. Perhaps talking to a professional counselor can help you resolve some of your problems.

SPIRITUALITY: Some of the pain and emptiness you feel is due to a loss of spiritual vitality. By forgiving yourself and others, you find your way to divine grace.

EMPOWERMENT: Pick up the pieces and move forward.

SIX OF CUPS

Old memories and new opportunities, childhood, children, nostalgia, and generally happy times form the heart of this card. Skills and abilities that haven't been used for a while are likely to be resurrected. A missed opportunity needs to be reconsidered; past efforts bring future rewards.

Are you passing up current and future chances for success because you prefer to dwell on past glory? If recollections of triumphs on your college's football field or popularity as a high school cheerleader fill you with nostalgia, rethink your current situation. Once you begin to believe that your best years are behind you, that will become your reality.

IN A READING: Remember the wishes and dreams of your childhood. Use those memories in your creative work. Someone or something from the past comes to your aid and provides inspiration and new energy. Don't allow wistful yearnings for things that probably never were to obscure your current goals.

Children and children's issues are also highlighted. This can refer to children in general, your own children, a teacher, a mentor, or a happy family event.

WORK: Creative occupations are enriched by the happy fantasies of childhood or the past in general. Painting, poetry, filmmaking, and fiction writing meet with financial and critical success. You receive royalties or win an award for past efforts. Someone you worked with in the past resurfaces in your life and offers a new opportunity.

ROMANCE: An old lover suddenly shows up on your doorstep and the chemistry is rekindled. A chance encounter with a childhood friend brings extremely favorable news or fulfills a romantic fantasy.

FINANCES: Your old toys and other childhood treasures bring money on the nostalgia market. Invest in companies that cater to children and to childhood fantasy and romantic dreams, such as theme parks, movie studios, travel agencies, antique shops, and art galleries.

HEALTH: Make sure that your new doctor gets a copy of your medical records. Physical or emotional problems surfacing now probably have roots in your past. You benefit from hypnosis or past-life therapy as a means of tapping into unconscious memories. A visit to a place that has tugged at you all of your life results in a remission.

SPIRITUALITY: You recall the warmth and safety you found in childhood beliefs and family rituals. This could lead you back to the church or synagogue of your youth or on to new beliefs and rituals through the study of mythology and the Old Religion.

EMPOWERMENT: Revive, recycle, reuse. You find current answers in forgotten skills, old dreams, and unlived fantasies.

SEVEN OF CUPS

Imagination and fantasy combine to produce numerous opportunities. You may have myriad options, but you feel muddled and confused and have trouble distinguishing the good choices from the bad. You need to make a choice and should devote much care and consideration to making it. What you desire most may be right under your nose, just waiting to be recognized.

IN A READING: Until you pick one of your alternatives and begin working with it, all your dreams and ideas remain just castles in the air. Beneath your confusion and indecision lies an abundance of innovative energy waiting to be released.

WORK: For an artist, actor, writer, or filmmaker, daydreaming and fantasy result in new ideas. In business, however, you need to be more practical and to narrow your choices. This seven sometimes warns of dubious behavior, sham transactions, and dirty deals: In short, beware the snake-oil salesman.

ROMANCE: You're vacillating in your search for a lover or a mate. The heady intoxication of falling in love with love leads to sobering disappointment. Focus on what you want, evaluate your numerous choices, then decide what (or who) you really want.

FINANCES: That investment that looks so lucrative could be a mirage. Be careful where you place your trust and money. A reliable financial advisor can help you sort out your options and separate the genuine opportunity from the deception.

HEALTH: Your medical doctor can't find anything wrong with you and your analyst has written you off as a hopeless escapist. You really want to try alternative therapy, but you can't decide which one. You're not sick, you're just a little spacey. Start a dream journal. Surround yourself with grounding influences such as black tourmaline, obsidian, black onyx, or smokey quartz crystal.

SPIRITUALITY: The mysticism and idealism of this seven recalls the diversity of the many paths of New Age philosophy. You sample and explore everything: dreams, out-of-body experiences, meditation, yoga, candle magic, tarot, astrology, runes, aromatherapy, crystal healing. You derive a different type of spiritual nourishment from each one.

EMPOWERMENT: Manifest your dreams by using creative visualization to focus on specific goals and bring them into physical reality.

EIGHT OF CUPS

You're leaving the past behind. You abandon a situation because of disappointment, disillusionment, or merely because things have reached their natural conclusion. Unlike the five of cups, which usually means that someone has left you, the eight indicates that you voluntarily turn away from a dying relationship or an unfulfilling job or career.

Traditionally, this card is connected to the Hermit. You may decide to put the things of ordinary life behind you in order to devote yourself to the search for wisdom and enlightenment.

IN A READING: You're leaving a situation that no longer works. It's a conscious decision, based on a sense of stagnation and the need to experience other things.

You're feeling blue or fatigued, suffering the effects of this in-between stage when you've completed a life phase and are waiting for new inspiration or energy. You may experience a gradual withdrawal of affection or a loss of interest in a relationship.

WORK: You've gone as far as you can go in your current job or career. Although you're not quite sure which way to go, you're ready to try to something new. Put out feelers, let friends know you're looking for something new, talk to a headhunter. You may decide to bow out of the nine-to-five world altogether and seek something that feeds your soul.

ROMANCE: You reach a fork in the road. A long-term relationship is ending and you're prepared to head off in a new direction. Even though you feel sad about separating from someone who has meant a lot to you, you're eager to move on with your life.

FINANCES: Your financial problems and commitments seem monumental, but you're ready to let go of the comforts of a secure job. Once you sever the cord, new possibilities and opportunities open up and you embark on a new financial path that is more in line with your beliefs. This might entail investing in earth-friendly companies.

HEALTH: The insecurity of not knowing what the future holds plays havoc with your health. You experience periods of depression, stress, and uncertainty. But you're moving in the right direction. Refuse to become discouraged, pull yourself out of the blues, and nurture a belief in your body's ability to heal itself.

SPIRITUALITY: You find depth of meaning in solitude. Your inward turning is directly related to the changes in your life. In stillness and meditation, you forge a new link with your higher self. Your spiritual quest begins alone, out of need, and through it you open yourself to all that has been lacking in your life.

EMPOWERMENT: You follow your inner voice toward new horizons.

NINE OF CUPS

The wish card is the fairy godmother of the tarot. It portends happiness, contentment, fulfillment, abundance, material success, and physical well-being. A wish you have in some area of your life is answered.

The astrological correspondence to this card is Jupiter, known as "greater fortune." However, like Jupiter, it sometimes indicates too much of a good thing and laziness and overindulgence in sensual pleasures.

IN A READING: Your wish comes true, problems are behind you. Relax and enjoy a good time. Reward yourself for all the energy, time, and discipline you put into manifesting your dream. Appreciate the emotional satisfaction that comes with attaining one or more of your goals.

WORK: A delayed project now moves toward completion, but maybe not in the way you expected. A chance meeting or contact brings unexpected good fortune. Your book or script sells, your dream job lands in your lap.

ROMANCE: A synchronicity brings you the person you need at this point in your life. Sexual passion, sensual pleasures, or the deepening of commitment in an existing relationship fulfill you. You attend parties and gatherings and finally take a vacation that you've postponed.

FINANCES: Trust your luck. You may win the lottery or hit the jackpot in Las Vegas, but even if you don't, count on some kind of financial gain. Your business expands, your opportunities manifest in unpredictable and fortunate ways.

HEALTH: Your inner contentment infuses your body and mind with positive energy. By avoiding self-indulgence, rejecting surface values and quick-fix solutions, you ensure your continued physical well-being.

SPIRITUALITY: Open yourself to your innate ability to envision future events. Use creative visualization to mold and change what you see to fit your personal vision and worldview.

EMPOWERMENT: You allow yourself to wish for what you want and trust that you will get it.

TEN OF CUPS

The happy family card represents joy and contentment in personal relationships. It's indicative of permanent, enduring success, complete happiness, emotional harmony, and prosperity.

The relationship symbolized by the two of cups has burgeoned into lasting love and expanded to include the entire family circle. The ten of cups refers primarily to domestic bliss, but it can appear in any situation where you've reached a high level of fulfillment and security.

IN A READING: You've achieved what you have been seeking and working toward. You finally feel safe and protected, and true happiness, rather than just the absence of pain, is your prize. Your friendly mood extends to neighbors and business contacts. Gratitude prompts you to give something back to the community. Through cooperation and teamwork all areas of your life improve and prosper.

WORK: Past difficulties fade, crises subside, and harmony reigns in your associations with coworkers and superiors. Social and family contacts bring in new clients or customers. A contract or agreement finally comes through. You manage to combine work with a family vacation and everyone comes home feeling refreshed.

ROMANCE: The focus is on true love, commitment, and marriage. If you're still single, it dawns on you that the person you're with is the one, and you pop the question. If you're married, you renew your vows or rededicate yourself to your significant other and your life together.

FINANCES: New connections improve your business; your financial outlook is excellent. The family business prospers because it finally comes into its own. You're grateful for the support you're getting and reciprocate by helping out someone in need.

HEALTH: Vast improvement. Your physical problems disappear. A new sense of peace and well-being suffuse you.

SPIRITUALITY: Gratitude is the heart of your spiritual power. You join together with your peers and express appreciation of divine gifts. Filled with rapture, you bless the harvest and give thanks for life's miracles.

EMPOWERMENT: Fulfilled in your personal relations, you feel happy and secure in the embrace of your family and the people you love the most.

Pentacles

Issues: material possessions, money, prosperity, manifestation, health

Astrological element: earth

Season: autumn

ACE OF PENTACLES

This ace is about positive rewards for hard work. As the harbinger of fresh starts in all areas having to do with business and finance, it stands for worldly status, achievement, material gain, prosperity, and success.

The association of the suit of pentacles to the earth, the element of the body, connects it to physical health, proper diet, and nutrition.

IN A READING: You begin a venture that brings positive financial changes down the road. The timing is right. Don't be afraid to initiate a plan that seems a bit risky. The money you invest now will come back to you with interest.

You build a home or upgrade your existing home. You buy

property for speculative purposes. Something new is emerging in your life and it may be a child.

WORK: You hit upon the long-sought solution to a troubling professional problem. A raise, promotion, a new job, or a career change is in store for you. You shouldn't have to move to take the job unless the surrounding cards indicate it. You're in the right place at the right time. Run with it.

ROMANCE: A romantic partnership benefits you in emotional and material ways. You meet someone new or discover new ways to develop and improve an existing relationship. You and your significant other may go into business together doing something you've both longed to do. But you call the shots.

FINANCES: New business and financial opportunities charge into your life. Your investments begin to pay off. You're offered much more than you expected for a piece of property you've held on to for years. If you decide to sell your home, you won't have to wait long for a buyer and you get what you ask for it. You accrue whatever you value: money, prestige, personal satisfaction, long-term security.

HEALTH: You're on the road to recovery. To speed things along, you may decide to consult an herbalist or a practitioner of crystal healing. Consider vacationing at a spa that offers an all-vegetarian regimen, mineral and mud baths, outdoor exercise, and time to commune with nature. Stick to a physical exercise program.

SPIRITUALITY: Meditation helps to ground you. You benefit spiritually from work connected to ecology, herbs, alternative medicine.

EMPOWERMENT: You have the power to manifest your plans, ideas, and dreams.

TWO OF PENTACLES

Think balance, adaptability, and equilibrium. You juggle a number of different projects and sources of income. This may entail working two jobs or handling full-time employment as you attend school. However, you don't feel overburdened because pleasure is inherent to your pursuits.

IN A READING: You strike a balance, but you do it with the cheer and enthusiasm of a juggler in a vaudeville act. There's a hidden magic in the way you maintain your equilibrium. You may be balancing a variety of projects or harmonizing inner spiritual development with outer material growth. Avoid spreading yourself too thin. If necessary, narrow your choices to maintain a balanced disposition.

WORK: Travel relates to your job and profession. Travel plans, however, may be delayed by niggling glitches, but you'll eventually get to where you want to be. As a confirmed multitasker, you're flexible and capable of balancing a number of complex projects and ideas at once. Don't hoard your energy; now is the time to take a calculated risk.

ROMANCE: You and your significant other are probably trying to squeeze time for each other from your hectic schedules. If you've planned a weekend away together, it may take considerable readjustments in your plans to pull it off. But once you do, it's worth it; passion is rekindled. A major change ushers in a new era for the relationship.

FINANCES: You balance the books through skillful manipulation. Money goes out as fast as it comes in, but you're satisfied because the bills are paid. Your financial situation is fluid enough to keep everything moving. Your small business gets a needed break from an interested investor. You may even take a portion of your profits and invest in an earth-friendly company.

HEALTH: Expect a round of medical tests. Ultimately, the news is good; most of your stiffness, aches, and pains are stress related. Yoga, stretching, and aerobic exercise help you blow off tension and maintain an upbeat mental outlook.

SPIRITUALITY: By reading books with spiritual themes, you open yourself to new possibilities. You begin to accept the holistic view that mind, body, emotions, and spirit are intimately connected. What affects one, affects the other. You draw spiritual nourishment from the daily aspects of your life.

EMPOWERMENT: Your versatility is your greatest strength.

THREE OF PENTACLES

As a journeyman or master builder, you've reached the end of your educational or developmental phase. You've passed the necessary tests and have earned your degree, license, or title. While the eight of pentacles typifies the apprentice, the three symbolizes someone who is a virtuoso in his or her field. Your expertise in the area for which you are qualified garners monetary rewards and public recognition.

IN A READING: You're entering into new realms of experience in your chosen career. This is a step up, not a change of course. It's what you have been working toward. When you're called upon to present evidence of your craftsmanship, skill, and knowledge, you respond brilliantly and are recognized publicly.

WORK: Professional recognition puts you in line for a well-earned promotion. If you're working on a writing project—a book, lecture, or presentation—you may have to fine-tune it. But the basics are done, the foundation is laid, and you sell your project.

ROMANCE: Personal relationships mature. You and your significant other resolve past problems and differences and achieve a new level of intimacy and loyalty. You may purchase a home together or renovate the place where you live now.

FINANCES: If you made a loan way back when, it's repaid with interest. A check arrives for royalties, residuals, interest on CDs and money markets, or option money on a creative project. You're spending money on renovations: new carpets, a fresh coat of paint, maybe new furniture. Call it perfectionism or attention to detail, but you keep adding new ideas in an attempt to improve the quality of the work. Ultimately you may need to enlist the aid of others to help you complete the project.

HEALTH: You may need to undergo medical tests. Your doctor is a top person in his/her field, someone who inspires total confidence. The news is good: Your condition isn't serious. Any treatment you need will be state of the art.

SPIRITUALITY: You're initiated into the older mysteries or a secret society, guild, or fraternity. As a seeker on a path of wisdom and spiritual growth, you quickly become an adept in mysticism, "magick" or the occult.

EMPOWERMENT: You use your skills and abilities to create something beautiful and enduring.

FOUR OF PENTACLES

You want a strong financial base and you're willing to compromise your higher aspirations to attain it. You tend to be possessive, holding on to what is yours. Even though you work hard to reach your goals, your accomplishments don't bring you the satisfaction you crave.

Don't be afraid of change, and guard against clinging to the status quo. It could attract disaster. Open yourself to new ideas and the opinions of others.

IN A READING: You're clinging to what is familiar: a job, material possessions, a relationship, or a certain safe environment. You know that your fixed ideas of security and safety are holding you back from fulfillment, but right now you're too scared to change. You abhor extravagance and waste and know how to make every penny count. You believe that a certain amount of selfishness concerning your time or financial resources is needed to build a solid financial foundation.

WORK: You take a job you don't like because it keeps the wolf from your door. After a while, your myopia prompts you to forget that other possibilities and paths are open to you. The bills are paid and your discontent seems preferable to the uncertainty of an unfamiliar or risky opportunity. But this phase is transitory; you're actually laying the foundation for future success.

ROMANCE: Chances are you're holding on to a relationship that no longer works. Or perhaps you're repeating old patterns in a new relationship. No matter how miserable you are, your deep-rooted fear of abandonment causes you to cling to a relationship that hasn't worked for some time.

FINANCES: This card sometimes points to a miserly disposition. Even when you're financially stable and secure, you're extremely protective of your wealth and possessions. Loosen up. Abundance is infinite.

HEALTH: The state of your health is bound up with your attitudes and beliefs about money and financial security. What symptoms are you clinging to? What emotions should you release? You benefit more from psychological counseling than from medical attention. You need to learn how and when to let go. Once you do, your constipation vanishes and your migraines are history.

SPIRITUALITY: Find your inner comfort zone and use it as a starting point for chakra meditation. Act on the images and impulses you receive. After all, these messages are coming from the deepest levels of your being.

EMPOWERMENT: You make every effort count and don't allow anything to go to waste.

FIVE OF PENTACLES

The news isn't good. You've reached an unlucky impasse that produces financial crisis, temporary hardship, and insecurity. Unemployment or heavy debts pull you down. A costly illness may be involved. Your world feels shaky right now. You keep wondering when the whole thing is going to collapse completely.

This five often addresses freelance work and self-employment that tends toward feast or famine. It also relates to the apprehension you feel when changing your job or occupation. It reflects those growth situations where outsiders can't help you and you must stand or fall on your own.

IN A READING: You aren't really suffering, but you've accustomed yourself to the belief that you are. Emotionally, you feel out in the cold, ignored and abandoned by those close to you. Physically, you need to pay more attention to your health. Your mind is focused on survival issues. Inertia threatens. Stop worrying. Mobilize your energy toward positive goals.

WORK: You're unemployed, underemployed, or about to lose your job. Filled with feelings of apprehension and self-doubt, you don't know where to turn. Difficult dealings with business associates and differences over contracts and agreements increase the stress and tension you experience. Step back and try to view the situation dispassionately.

ROMANCE: There's a lack in your relationship, a spiritual impoverishment. Your significant other holds different religious convictions than you do. If the two of you manage to stick together through the hard times, you may discover a depth of love for each other that you didn't know was there.

FINANCES: Brace yourself for tough times. You're in for business and financial setbacks. If you consider filing for bankruptcy, don't rush into it. Give yourself time to think it through. Review your remaining assets with an eye toward the future. Reconsider options you've previously rejected.

HEALTH: A physical problem needs attention, but it isn't as bad as you think. Financial and emotional issues play havoc with your life and cause worry, strain, and anxiety. Once you tone down the stress level and learn to deal with your problems, your health rebounds.

SPIRITUALITY: Stressed-out and bone-tired, you feel as if you've fallen from a state of grace. You could use some inspiration or guidance in spiritual matters, but no one seems to be able to help you. You're going to have to find your way alone. Begin with purifying, cleansing, and rebalancing rituals. Prepare yourself for the new opportunity as a farmer prepares his ground for seeding.

EMPOWERMENT: You've hit bottom and are ready to pull yourself back up. Hold on and your fortunes will reverse.

SIX OF PENTACLES

Assistance is available. One way or another life conspires to provide you with what you need. You don't win the lottery, but you get a push in the right direction. The support you receive is not strictly financial; your ideas and efforts meet with comprehension and approval. Open yourself to the magical forces that allow you to generously give or receive aid when necessary. Be alert for synchronicities.

IN A READING: You've rounded a critical bend and are headed for something better. Worthwhile ideas and projects are rewarded with a bonus or a raise. Your struggles are waning, help is at hand. This assistance may be a loan, a social security check, financial aid for school, a scholarship, gift, inheritance, or even a business proposition.

WORK: The project you recently launched is successful. Your bank loan is approved. A wealthy backer steps in to help with start-up expenses. Suddenly, the seemingly impossible becomes possible.

ROMANCE: You and your significant other comfort and support each other. It's an equitable relationship in which you both give and receive according to your capabilities. Tokens of love and affection are exchanged. If you're not involved, you meet someone special through a support group; he or she may work in the health field.

FINANCES: Your request for disability, VA benefits, SSI, welfare, a grant, profit-sharing distribution, or pension money comes through. A debt is repaid. Your small-business loan or mortgage is approved. Overall, your finances improve through the intervention of a third party.

HEALTH: A healing occurs. Someone gives you what you need in the form of touch therapy or the laying on of hands. Your medical bills are paid through insurance or the generosity of others. You round a critical bend.

SPIRITUALITY: An exchange of energy is indicated. You share your resources and advise those in need. On a higher level, this indicates that you pass along your healing power, wisdom, and/or worldly goods without hesitation. What you give to others comes back to you twofold.

EMPOWERMENT: By sharing with others, you attract whatever you need.

SEVEN OF PENTACLES

It's time to take stock. Evaluate your achievements and trust that the projects you've set in motion can now move forward under their own momentum. You may be tempted to rest on your laurels for a while, but the pause won't last long. Your inspiration urges you on.

Through honest appraisal of your needs and desires, you attune yourself to deeper levels of awareness and take your cues from synchronicities, hunches, impulses.

IN A READING: You have what it takes. Your hard work is about to pay off financially. You feel pride and fulfillment in what you've done and now you reflect on where you've been and where you would like to go. You reevaluate your goals, relationships, lifestyle, and dreams, and decide that you've done just fine so far. Buoyed by your past success, you charge into the future.

WORK: You may be offered a promotion or a raise only to discover that you prefer to move on to something entirely new and different. You opt for an extended leave or a long vacation. Even if you do nothing more than work in your garden, you replenish yourself for what lies ahead.

ROMANCE: You review and reevaluate your close personal relationships. The process itself is as important as the conclusions you reach. If you're uninvolved, you examine your current situation and take steps to make major lifestyle changes.

FINANCES: Even if the momentum of what you're trying to achieve falters or briefly wanes, keep moving. Take a risk. Innovative changes in your investment portfolio will be rewarded. Patience pays off. Royalties or unexpected sales on old projects tide you through a transition.

HEALTH: You may have to deal with ailments you've had before. But you're better equipped now to cope, and, through belief work, you achieve a period of physical and mental wellbeing. You're so pleased with the results of your medical checkup, you decide to follow it up with a sensible new diet and exercise plan.

SPIRITUALITY: Through honest, detached appraisal of your life as it is now, at this moment, you break through negative beliefs. You realize that life unfolds from the inside out, not the other way around. You attend a workshop or seminar on manifestation, and the results astound you.

EMPOWERMENT: Your hard work pays off. You benefit from time out before moving on to your next project.

EIGHT OF PENTACLES

The focus here is on education—workshops or lectures you attend to hone your skills, or actual enrollment in a full-time program where you work toward a degree. You can turn a talent, hobby, or interest into a new career. You're an apprentice now and love every second of it.

IN A READING: You tackle a long-term task with excellent future prospects. Although you're still in the apprentice stage, you're hired for a job that requires more advanced knowledge and expertise. Your employer sends you to school or provides on-the-job training. Hard work and practical ideas have got you this far; good luck carries you the rest of the way.

WORK: A raise, new projects, and new responsibilities test your skills. You could be called upon to take on an assignment in an unfamiliar area. Although you have little previous knowledge to bring to this enterprise, you do well. Your interest, enthusiasm, and willingness to learn make up for your lack of experience.

ROMANCE: Pay attention to the small considerations which enhance a relationship. In an ongoing relationship, new experiences open up that deepen your bond with your partner. If you're not involved, you meet someone in a class or on campus during a seminar or workshop.

FINANCES: Financial assistance comes through for your studies. Backing for a new project or business is approved. Sit tight with regard to your investments; this isn't a good time to attempt major financial changes.

HEALTH: All the alterations in your life cause you to feel somewhat uncomfortable or slightly off balance. Your energy is low. Get more rest than you usually do, take vitamins, pay extra attention to your diet. You may have trouble with your teeth, your gums, or your digestive tract. It's all related to the imbalance you're experiencing. Try natural remedies to correct the problems.

SPIRITUALITY: Your journey begins with practicing the zen of day-to-day living. You finally understand that your point of power lies in the present, in the Now. The process is what matters. For now, reinforce this discovery in whatever way you can: through books, workshops, classes, or simply in the magnificent nuances of daily life.

EMPOWERMENT: You take great pride in everything you do and it shows.

NINE OF PENTACLES

You achieve material comfort, financial security, and a sense of inner peace. You enjoy relationships, but when you're alone, you're not lonely. You relish the personal environment you've created: your home, your garden, your pets, and comfortable lifestyle. You don't depend upon constant companionship to make you feel complete.

IN A READING: Financial protection and security allow you to use your resources to create a harmonious home and office environment. You find immense pleasure in gardening and in beautifying your surroundings. Self-reliance is the key to your prosperity; you follow your own star. Pleased that you are able to make your own way based on talent and ability, you are nonetheless thrilled when recognized or praised for your accomplishments.

WORK: An employment opportunity drops in your lap, an unexpected partnership is formed, or the promotion of a product or project you've launched exceeds your wildest expectations. If you're in the arts or self-employed, you're now in a position that's comfortable enough financially so you don't have to take on projects that don't interest you.

ROMANCE: Your relationship with your significant other is headed for smooth sailing, ease, and comfort. When circumstances force you to spend time apart, absence deepens your bond. If you're not involved, you meet someone through work or business; things between you click immediately.

FINANCES: Pursue real-estate investments or improvements to properties you own. Decorating and landscaping increase the value of your current home. Upgrade your furniture, paint and polish your house. Add a beautiful garden, put in a patio, pool, and spa. In money matters, trust yourself and follow your instincts. Everything you touch now turns to gold.

HEALTH: Vast improvement, particularly if you've recently undergone surgery, or have had nagging physical problems. Seek answers to your minor health questions in self-help books. Time alone, surrounded by your gardens and pets, your books and dreams, works wonders.

SPIRITUALITY: You undergo a change in consciousness and break through to a higher understanding of your inner riches. You embark on a solitary path of healing magic, plying your art in isolation. Dreams, meditation, channeling, and writing figure prominently in your journey.

EMPOWERMENT: You are your own best friend.

TEN OF PENTACLES

Known as the Wall Street card, the focus is on financial prosperity and firm foundations for home and family life. It points to transactions involving millions of dollars, an abrupt, better change in your living status, and the buying and selling of property. You enter a prosperous time of life.

There may be travel connected to work and business. On another level this card reminds us of the magic that lies just beneath the surface of everyday life.

IN A READING: You've entered a carefree phase suffused with abundance and stability. However, the happiness and contentment that you feel extend beyond material prosperity. Your health is good, your family life is stable. You're ready to move forward in the company of a group, corporation, or community. Consolidate your gains and expand your holdings.

WORK: You've achieved job security and an important place within your organization. You're "making it" and your success is well deserved. Don't be afraid to take risks to build on what you have achieved. If you've longed to be self-employed, then now is the time to pursue that dream.

ROMANCE: There's a rich emotional bond between you and your significant other. Everything clicks between you, almost as if you're of one mind, one soul. If you're uninvolved, you soon meet someone while traveling for business or through work-related events. Don't go looking; the relationship will find you.

FINANCE: You inherit a substantial amount of money, receive a windfall from stocks or other investments, or make a killing on a real-estate deal. Invest part of your profits in new projects and properties; now is the time to build on what you've gained.

HEALTH: Your physical and emotional health take a definite turn for the better. If you pet is ailing, a trip to the vet turns up minor problems that are solved through a change in diet.

SPIRITUALITY: Concentrate on the hidden experience in ordinary things. Through the richness of your daily life, you gain something beyond material success. You're in tune with your higher self and experience incidents of clairvoyance, clairaudience, and precognitive dreams.

EMPOWERMENT: Abundance is your reward for learning how to manifest your desires on the physical plane.

Swords

Issues: intellect, left-brain thinking, strife and challenges, ideas that are about to appear in your life

Astrological element: air

Season: winter

ACE OF SWORDS

Strength in adversity is the hallmark of this ace. You use all of your willpower, courage, and intellect to reach your goals. However, its double edge means that it cuts both ways; the result of its power and energy may be destructive as well as constructive. Understanding comes to you by cutting through illusion and peeling away the layers of a situation to get to the core of the truth.

IN A READING: You begin to think and communicate differently. New ideas and beliefs prompt you to invent something, to find the answer to a mystery, or to resolve an old problem. You're able to seize the initiative and take advantage of new opportunities. No matter what the odds, you get what you want.

WORK: Innovative ideas sweep through your mind like a fresh breeze. Obsolete techniques and outmoded procedures are replaced with state-of-the-art techniques. Your decisive mood makes it easy to resolve misunderstandings and clear the decks for new projects.

ROMANCE: Emotional extremes are indicated. A sudden romance or an intense sexual encounter may take you by surprise. Or a previously warm relationship may suddenly turn cold. You're ready to cut the ties that bind if you feel your freedom threatened.

FINANCES: Remove the dead wood from your investment portfolio. Use your intellect to analyze your financial situation and then make the necessary changes. A problem may arise with someone who owes you money and can't afford to repay you.

HEALTH: You need to find ways to release the pressure of pent-up emotions, stress, and anxiety. Physical activity is the panacea you've been looking for. Join a gym, hire a personal trainer, or create an exercise program you can live with. Whichever plan you follow, working out on a daily basis helps to bring your physical and mental energy into balance.

SPIRITUALITY: This ace relates to the destruction of illusion in the search for understanding. It allows you to use your intellect to pierce the veil of the material universe and uncover spiritual truths.

EMPOWERMENT: You overcome obstacles by applying your willpower and intellect to problem solving.

TWO OF SWORDS

You've reached the proverbial fork in the road and don't know which path to take. You keep procrastinating about your choice because there's something about the situation you refuse to see. A temporary truce or compromise may be in place, but the problem still exists. Sooner or later you must make a decision to end the stalemate.

IN A READING: You're immobilized by your own fear and it has brought you to an impasse. Ignoring your problem won't make it go away. The time has come to choose. By acting swiftly and decisively you can turn the situation to your advantage. Sometimes the choice that's hanging you up has to be made by others.

WORK: You're caught in the middle of a negotiation that has reached a standstill. There seems to be no satisfactory course of action that will break the deadlock. If necessary, call in an unbiased third party to help settle the remaining differences. If you're waiting for an answer about a job interview, college application, or a similar query, this card is telling you the results aren't in yet. Be patient.

ROMANCE: You and your partner are involved in an uneasy truce regarding a major life issue. If you can't come up with a mutually satisfactory solution, then take a break from each other. Head out by yourself for a weekend, make plans with friends you haven't seen for a while, go to a movie alone. What you do isn't as important as doing *something*.

FINANCES: Your monetary concerns are justified. Collections are at a standstill and you must move off dead center to get the cash flowing again. To resolve these problems quickly, you may have to force the issue. Your credit obligations have brought you to an impasse. Take stock, then act.

HEALTH: Blocked emotions are causing you to feel tense and out of sorts. By denying your true feelings, you've thrown your entire system out of balance. Fear and uncertainty about the future add to the sensation of imbalance and insecurity. Those medical test results you're waiting for will probably be delayed.

SPIRITUALITY: By practicing Tai Chi, you regain your mental balance and sense of inner peace. On a deeper level, meditation allows you to temporarily withdraw from your worldly concerns. Breathing exercises help put you into the proper frame of mind so that you can decide what you want to do next.

EMPOWERMENT: You've got a decision to make and once you've made it your life will resume its forward momentum.

THREE OF SWORDS

Heartbreak, loss, disappointment: The news hurts. Your suffering can be quite literal, as in the pain of a heart attack. Your painful experience also may refer to the emotional aftermath of a broken relationship.

One way or another, intense feelings take their toll and cause you deep distress. These feelings could be the result of a crisis stemming from a romantic triangle, an abusive situation, codependency, or longstanding problems between lovers.

IN A READING: It may become necessary to remove the cause of your pain through cardiac surgery, divorce, or separation. Letting go of what no longer serves your best interests is sometimes the only way to end your pain. You probably feel that all is lost, but remember the adage: "This too shall pass." Then the real healing will begin.

WORK: Whether you like it or not, changes must be made. As a manager, you'll downsize your operation by terminating employees and cutting down on spending. For a writer, a rejection of your manuscript results in drastic editing and rewrites. Inspiration leads you far afield of your original ideas. Some projects may need to be scrapped and others totally revamped.

ROMANCE: You've experienced enough heartache. Face facts and end the connection that has brought you so much anguish. The pain you feel at parting is nothing compared to the ongoing unhappiness of a miserable relationship. If you're uncommitted but looking, don't be in a hurry. Evaluate the past patterns and the core beliefs that have brought you unhappiness and work on changing them.

FINANCES: Get rid of investments that haven't clicked. It's time to give up on disappointing properties and unproductive programs. Take your lumps and move on to healthier, more rewarding financial markets.

HEALTH: This three is connected to heart trouble and problems with the blood. Bypass surgery is a distinct possibility. With the Empress, ace of cups, or page of cups, a pregnancy may end in abortion or miscarriage.

SPIRITUALITY: Use your disappointments as stepping stones in your development. Look inside yourself for inspiration. Release old ideas and generate new ones. Surrender what you no longer need so there's room for the new order.

EMPOWERMENT: Acknowledge your pain, examine it, and work through it. Then let it go and move on.

FOUR OF SWORDS

Incarceration is the literal meaning of this card. It can mean a hospital stay, jail term, a period of rest and recuperation, or simply time out for quiet contemplation. Whatever form it takes, this four signifies a period of inactivity or convalescence and time away from your normal life.

IN A READING: Your strength is exhausted and circumstances conspire to force you to slow down or temporarily drop out and rest. For now you're stuck in neutral. This break in your activities is long overdue; use it to revitalize yourself. Take a vacation, go on a retreat, or just relax and get in touch with your inner self.

WORK: Activities stall, projects stagnate, nothing is happening. You feel disappointed, tired, and frustrated. You've reached a dead end and need to put some distance between yourself and your problems. Take time off or devote yourself to other projects. You'll return to your original purpose renewed and brimming with fresh ideas.

ROMANCE: Whether you lack intimacy or feel deserted within an existing relationship, you perceive yourself as isolated and alone. Either way, a romantic trip is just the ticket to meeting someone new or reviving a dying affair. On the other hand, you might decide to set your relationship issues aside for a while and take some time out to pamper yourself at a health resort or spa.

FINANCES: No news is not good news when progress is stalled and payments are long overdue. Step back and analyze your situation. This period of inactivity seems endless, but it won't last forever.

HEALTH: The need for physical or emotional healing is implicit in this card. If you haven't recovered completely from a previous illness, more rest may be required. Professional assistance can help you gain a better perspective. Consider psychotherapy if you can't work out your problems on your own.

SPIRITUALITY: Read, study, and educate yourself in the use of guided imagery and meditation. Attend a sweat-lodge ceremony, take some time off and do something that feeds your soul. Focus your power and allow it to tap into the healing energies and restorative capabilities of the universe.

EMPOWERMENT: Put all your concerns to one side and take time out. You'll emerge renewed and refreshed.

FIVE OF SWORDS

An empty victory is at hand. You win, but was it worth the effort? Is this what you really want? Examine your motives and ask yourself if you secretly wanted to lose in this situation. Perhaps you won the day by engaging in deception and unfair tactics. Perhaps these tactics were used against you. One way or another, this card reflects a confrontation that brings pain to both parties.

IN A READING: Sabotage or treachery may have a bearing on something that you're involved in. In spite of everything, you'll be able to confront issues head-on and solve your problems. Sometimes this card indicates escape from danger, the breaking of bonds, or a lifting of restrictions. If you're going to break out you will need to take some definitive action. Don't expect to sit around on your duff and have freedom handed to you on a silver platter.

WORK: You're in for a struggle, and you will get little help or compassion from others. This card sometimes relates to termination of employment followed by a court battle. In other circumstances you find that in the workplace you are your own worst enemy. Before you attack business associates, think of the inevitable consequences. Consider neutral arbitration by a third party as a viable alternative to all-out war.

ROMANCE: Domination of one person over the other can ruin any union. If you've been playing the heavy and taking advantage of your significant other, you'll soon find that you've lost more than you've gained. In the reverse situation, don't allow the other party to continue asserting power over you. Either way, the relationship has probably failed and will soon end unless you're both willing to compromise.

FINANCES: Your position is precarious. Things won't come easily and your well-laid plans may fail, so proceed with caution. If you're clear in your thinking and logical in your actions, you move through this difficult phase unscathed. Even if you're financially solvent, you still feel extremely nervous and uncertain about the future.

HEALTH: Be especially careful not to turn your feelings of anger and hostility against yourself. Guard against self-destructive activities that can ruin your health and undermine your sense of well-being. Channel your overaggressive tendencies into competitive sports and the martial arts.

SPIRITUALITY: Use your energy in the pursuit of a higher cause. But don't get sucked into the dubious position of fanatical crusader who tries to cram the "truth" down everyone else's throat.

EMPOWERMENT: When you encounter a no-win situation, acknowledge it and withdraw gracefully.

SIX OF SWORDS

Consider this card a metaphorical gateway through which you journey away from your problems. The move may be a literal one to a new home or office or a figurative journey that plays out solely on an inner level. Either way, it represents a turning point. Your situation improves.

IN A READING: Travel is indicated. You take an international trip, possibly by boat, or an overseas visitor comes to see you. Although all your troubles haven't ended, you're aware of a lessening of strain and tension. You've made certain decisions that are pushing you in a new direction. The future may be unknown, but you move toward it with hope in your heart.

WORK: You're leaving a well-known area for something new and different. Apprehension is natural whether you're moving your place of business or changing your job. It would be nice if you could hold on to your old life while testing your options, but that's not the way it works. Be prepared to distance yourself from the past. During this transition period, help comes from unexpected sources.

ROMANCE: A short pleasure trip with your spouse will accomplish more than a visit to a marriage counselor. If you're single, plan a cruise or vacation to distant shores. You're longing for different experiences, new places, fresh faces, and a chance to get away from it all.

FINANCES: A debt counselor devises a plan to restructure your finances. There may be some delays and setbacks, but ultimately you'll get that bill-consolidation loan you need.

HEALTH: You travel to a distant clinic, if necessary, for evaluation of a health problem. The rapport you establish with the doctors and nurses eases your tension. Your physical problems are resolved, but it doesn't happen overnight. Put your trust in those whose job it is to cure your dis-ease.

SPIRITUALITY: In your search, you journey through various levels of consciousness and study different belief systems. You pass with ease from the waking state to dreaming and back again.

EMPOWERMENT: You're putting distance between yourself and past difficulties.

SEVEN OF SWORDS

Don't allow others to take advantage of you. State your convictions and don't be browbeaten into doing what you don't want to do. When you're negotiating a deal, play your cards close to the chest, and you'll outsmart the opposition.

Mistrust and unnecessary secrecy are more likely to lead to isolation than to security. Although you need to guard against underhanded people, this suspicion can lead to paranoia if carried too far.

IN A READING: Take steps to protect your possessions; someone may be trying to rip you off. There's a daring act afoot designed to surprise or trick you with convoluted schemes and impulsive actions. Be prudent and evasive. To reach your objective, rely on your intellect and diplomacy. Nothing is accomplished by aggression.

WORK: As a manager, you're in danger of being embarrassed by an employee who shirks responsibility or tries to sneak away from certain duties. You may not want to believe the truth, especially if it means that you've been duped. Avoid office politics and rely upon your own shrewdness to uncover deception and duplicity. Ultimately, you get what you're entitled to, but you may have to go through the back door to do it.

ROMANCE: You would love to get closer to someone, but your lack of trust keeps him or her at a distance. You sidestep honest discussion in favor of insincere small talk, then wonder why the relationship keeps stalling. To the other person, it's obvious that you're hiding your true feelings. As long as you continue to beat around the bush, dodging the main issue, no agreement is possible.

FINANCES: When negotiating a deal you may have to give in on a number of details in order to get your major plans approved. Check out anyone who tries to involve you in a get-rich-quick scheme. Financial conditions are unstable, but you may stumble across an opportunity. Remain alert for synchronicities. Don't compromise your integrity.

HEALTH: Be wary of medical practitioners who prescribe numerous tests or unnecessary treatments. Get a second opinion before agreeing to any type of surgical intervention.

SPIRITUALITY: You're in danger of being cheated or deceived by an insincere or unscrupulous religious leader. Stay clear of cults or other groups that prey on those most in need of spiritual comfort.

EMPOWERMENT: You take the sting out of the opposition by keeping your strategy secret until you're ready to do battle.

EIGHT OF SWORDS

You're holding yourself back from living life to the fullest. You project your fears and inhibitions into your surroundings, then you view them as obstacles. The limitations you perceive don't lie in the outer world. They are projections of your own inner apprehension and anxiety. Paralyzed by fear of the unknown, you're afraid to break the chains that bind you. As long as you greet positive suggestions with expressions such as "I can't" and "Yes, but," nothing will change.

IN A READING: You feel as if you're in a mental prison, unable to find your way out of a situation. All exits seem to be blocked. You're eaten up with dread and insecurity. However, it's your fear of the unknown that holds you back. You've boxed yourself in and convinced yourself that you have no options.

Although you feel you're in an impossible situation, there *is* a way out. Remove your blinders and expand your ideas of what is possible.

WORK: Your feeling of frustration is monumental; you feel blocked at every turn. You say that you want out of an oppressive job or profession, but it appears as if you'd rather endure restriction than deal with your need to make a change. Deep down, you view your familiar difficulties and problems as protection against the unknown possibilities of the world at large.

ROMANCE: Although you feel restricted, you're afraid to break your bonds and cut yourself loose. Perhaps you're alone and lonely, or involved in an unproductive relationship. Either way, you refuse to see that you're holding yourself back.

FINANCES: You're stuck in a negative cycle of events. You need to make more money, but you're convinced that your bad luck is never going to end. The first step to conquering your fear is to take a hard look at your options.

HEALTH: Mental distress and a sense of hopelessness nag at you. You undergo medical tests for an undiagnosed condition. On a psychological level, you may be using illness as an escape from your frustration and inability to free yourself from an untenable situation.

SPIRITUALITY: You must go deep inside your psyche and seek the answer that will help you to break out of your self-imposed confinement. By recognizing that you've set your own limitations through your thoughts and beliefs, you take the first step out of the situation you've created.

EMPOWERMENT: Nothing prevents you from leaving an oppressive situation except your own negative beliefs. Change those beliefs and you'll change your life.

NINE OF SWORDS

Worry and anxiety are the literal meaning of this nine. You experience sleepless nights and stress-induced nightmares. Fear runs rampant and you're convinced that your situation will continue to deteriorate and will never change for the better.

Mental anguish and depression are often brought about by a parent's concern for his or her family. You may experience a deep sadness for the problems of the world in general.

IN A READING: You're suffering from intense anxiety. Although your sense of impending doom and disaster may be unfounded, your pain is very real. Apprehension and difficulty sleeping have left you vulnerable to feelings of hopelessness.

Even though the current situation is difficult, it's not as bad as you think. If you feel that you can't get through this alone, seek out some counseling or training in stress-management techniques.

WORK: Problems on the job have led to anxious nights and stressed-filled days. Meet the shadows in your life head-on. The only way out of your professional difficulties is through direct confrontation with your problems, real and imagined.

ROMANCE: You suspect your significant other of cheating, or lack of interest. Stop tormenting yourself with phantoms and fears and bring your doubts out into the open. Clear the air with a heart-to-heart talk before your suspicions destroy your relationship. Even if you're correct in your assumptions of infidelity or disinterest, the truth is preferable to the demons of your imagination.

FINANCES: Confusion surrounding financial issues fuels your sense of panic. However, you're allowing negative emotions to cloud your judgment. It's one thing to be cautious and quite another to allow yourself to become paralyzed by self-doubt.

HEALTH: It's important to find solutions to your problems so that the tension produced by your anxiety won't take a toll on your mental and physical health. Don't seek relief in drugs or alcohol; that will only compound the problem. Your night terrors may bubble up from the unconscious, but they can be fought off by your conscious mind.

SPIRITUALITY: If you're in the throes of a "dark night of the soul," it would be wise to talk things over with an advisor you trust. By wrestling with the devils of your imagination, you overcome them.

EMPOWERMENT: By acknowledging feelings of sorrow, disappointment, shame, and disillusion, you take the first step toward releasing them.

TEN OF SWORDS

You're facing forced change and the final resolution of a situation or the dramatic end of a cycle. You give up on a lost cause and get on with the true purpose of your life. Ultimately, you feel relieved, accept the inevitable, and move on.

IN A READING: Despite the usually harsh depiction of this card in most decks, it isn't about physical death. It's about endings, treachery, and misfortune. It usually spells the end of a relationship, situation, or a particular time in your life. You may feel as if you've been stabbed in the back by someone you trusted.

Your loss seems worse than it is because it's unexpected and ends something you've been counting on. Actually, the worst is over and now you need to clear out the dead wood before you can move forward.

WORK: You're forced to quit your job or are demoted or dismissed. You may be aware of having consciously chosen this change or you may have been pushed out through the betrayal or disloyalty of someone you trusted. Either way, this is an opportunity to change your life for the better. You've outgrown your current position and the time has come for you to move on.

ROMANCE: Someone you love has hurt you very badly and you're having trouble putting it behind you. You've made a mistake, taken a chance on love and lost. There's no choice now but to abandon the relationship and start over. The sooner you accept the fact that it's over, the easier it will be to get on with your life.

FINANCES: Bad advice brings a sudden reversal of fortune. At the very least, things move in a different direction than you anticipated. You feel paralyzed and unable to act on your own behalf. Cut your losses and come to terms with your reduced situation. Although the future appears grim, other solutions quickly appear.

HEALTH: You're displeased with the quality of your medical treatment. The new drug or procedure that you were counting on has not made you feel any better. It's time to either change doctors or try an alternative therapy such as herbal medicine, nutritional counseling, or acupuncture.

SPIRITUALITY: The death and rebirth of the spirit signal the end of one cycle and the beginning of another. This is connected at a deeper level to the ego's release of some idea to which it has been attached. You may even experience a sense of relief as one portion of your inner struggle comes to an end and you have no choice except to let go.

EMPOWERMENT: You've experienced disaster and survived. There's little left in life for you to fear.

6

The
Spreads

Back in the sixties, those of us who had discovered the *I Ching* spent endless hours debating the nuances of how it worked. Did we, for instance, have to ask a question before we tossed the coins or the yarrow sticks? Would the system work better if we used actual Chinese coins or would pennies do the job just as well? And what about those sticks, anyway? Were toothpicks permissible?

More than a quarter of a century later, the answers seem obvious and can be applied to any divination system, especially the tarot. You can pose a question or not pose a question. Your choice of decks is irrelevant as long as the deck you choose speaks to *you*. Some spreads will work for you, others won't.

The point is that the tarot, like the *I Ching* or palmistry or tea leaves, is part of a *belief system.* Spreads are as intrinsic to the tarot as hexagrams are to the *I Ching.* Both are about patterns. Decipher the patterns and you discover an answer.

We have provided an array of spreads that pertain to daily life and that span the spectrum from the physical and emotional lives we lead to the spiritual realms we seek.

People You Read For

Whether the people you read for pay you or not, they all want one thing: *answers.* The more accurate your answers are, the more satisfied the individual will be and the better you will feel about yourself as a tarot reader.

These spreads are designed to make it easier for you to obtain accurate answers about the areas that concern most people: work and professions, romance and relationships with family and friends, health, finances, and spiritual issues.

Many of the spreads evolved out of our working for psychic 900-lines. Despite the bad rep that 900-lines seem to have, one fact is indisputable: They are the toughest kinds of readings to do because you do them cold.

You have no body language or facial expressions to tell you whether you've hit anything that pertains to the person's life. Much of the time, the only verbal cue you have is the caller's greeting. Also, these people are paying nearly four dollars a minute for a reading. If you don't hit something in sixty seconds, the caller hangs up.

As a result, these spreads, particularly the shorter ones, are geared to obtaining concrete information *quickly.* Once you've done that, follow with a longer spread and provide the person with more esoteric insight into his or her life.

The beauty of the tarot is that it offers information on both the mundane and the esoteric levels. But the answers are only as good as the reader. Use your intuition. Allow yourself to open up. Let the cards speak to you.

Traditional Versus Nontraditional Spreads

Page through any tarot book at your local bookstore and you'll find examples of traditional spreads. The Celtic Cross, the Horoscope spread, and the three-card past/present/future spreads are the most common. When you're just starting out, traditional spreads are excellent vehicles for learning the cards and developing an ease in using them. But at some point, you may discover limitations to these spreads or find that you need diversity. For us, the turning point was the 900-line. We desperately needed spreads that provided more specific information.

At one time, we rarely used the Celtic Cross. It seemed too complicated for most of the readings we were doing. But we've since realized that when we aren't getting any feedback and we don't know if we're on the right track or not, this spread pulls information out of the void.

Designing Your Own Spreads

Keep it simple in the beginning, using no more than three or four cards. Assign specific meanings to the positions. Play around with the placement until you find a design that feels right for that particular spread.

For instance, with a three-card spread do you want the cards in a straight line? A triangle? Two at the top and one at the bottom? Vice versa? The best spreads are those that evolve from your own questions and needs. Sometimes you'll get ideas from what other people are doing with tarot, and one of the best ways to do that is to log on to one of the electronic networks.

All of the larger networks have New Age sections that include tarot areas and most are very active. People post spreads, discuss cards, hold workshops, and do free readings online. Drop by and introduce yourself!

Difficult Combinations

To weave a spread into a story, you have to be able to read cards in combinations. This comes with practice. The meanings of some card combinations will be obvious to you. Let's say you want to know whether you're going to get that promotion you're after and draw the nine of wands, the Tower, and the six of wands.

In combination, these cards indicate that you should expect one final test, perhaps another interview. The job may involve some facet of television or other electronic media. Something unexpected (the Tower) happens before or during the interview that convinces you that you aren't going to be hired. The outcome, however, looks promising—victory after travails.

You draw two more cards to find out what the unexpected occurrence is and pull the five of swords and the three of pentacles. These two cards suggest there will be dissension and disagreement about your salary.

Other combinations, however, won't be as obvious. You may have to do several spreads to obtain the full picture.

About the Spreads

There are more than one hundred spreads in this section. It begins with the simplest (one card) and proceeds to the most complex (twenty-four).

When you're going through the spreads for the first time, keep your journal handy and record the results of any spreads that you try. You'll quickly discover which spreads feel right to you. This is also a way to build self-confidence, because you'll have a record of your hits.

One-Card Spreads

A CARD A DAY

Each morning, draw a single card to express the tone of that particular day. Interpret the card in your journal, then check it that evening to see how accurate the card was.

This is where you will begin to develop your own meanings for the cards. If your meanings differ from the other people's meanings, don't worry about it. Use what works for you.

You may find that you glean more information about what's coming up by using just majors.

YES/NO SPREAD

For any yes/no question, use the major arcana cards, the nine of cups, and four aces. The aces are for timing, all others are for yes, no, or can go either way. If the nine of cups comes up, it's a resounding *yes*. Otherwise use the list below as a guideline.

YES

Fool	Justice
Magician	Star
Empress	Sun
Emperor	World
Chariot	Nine of cups

CAN GO EITHER WAY

High Priestess	Hierophant
Wheel of Fortune	Moon
Lovers	Judgment

NO

Strength	Hanged Man
Tower	Death
Temperance	Devil
Hermit	

Two-Card Spreads

ENERGY SPREAD

1) The energy you'll be dealing with today (or tomorrow or next week)
2) How you can transmute this energy so that it works for you

EVERYDAY SPREAD

1) Events: refers to the types of events that may transpire today
2) Feelings: how you may feel or react to today's events

Three-Card Spreads

BODY/MIND/SPIRIT SPREAD

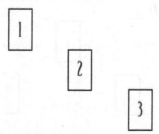

1) Body: how you're doing physically
2) Mind: how you're doing mentally
3) Spirit: how you're doing spiritually

DAILY SPREAD

1) The dominant energy for the day
2) How you'll feel about it/others who might be involved
3) How it affects you

FAST SOLUTION

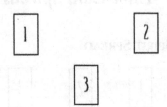

1) The nature of your problem
2) The cause of your problem
3) The solution to your problem

NANCY'S SPREAD

(Nancy Pickard)

1) Mental
2) Heart/soul
3) Spiritual

PAST/PRESENT/FUTURE SPREAD

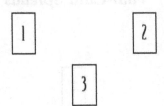

1) What happened in the past
2) What is happening now
3) What may happen in the future

WHAT YOU GET SPREAD

1) What you have
2) What you need to know
3) What you get

WHAT'S HAPPENING SPREAD

1) The event
2) What you need to know about this event
3) Its ultimate effect on you

QUICKIE 3

1) The issue, the root of the question
2) Present circumstances
3) Future

Four-Card Spreads

DESIRE SPREAD

1) What you have
2) What you desire
3) What you need
4) What you get

EVOLUTION SPREAD

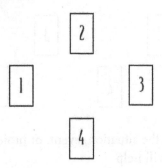

1) The situation as it exists now
2) How the situation will evolve in the next four weeks
3) Someone or something that will affect the situation
4) The outcome

FOUR WINDS SPREAD

(Based on the Inca Medicine Wheel as interpreted by Rob MacGregor)

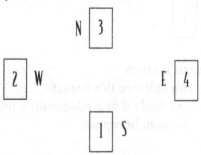

1) What you need to leave behind, to release
2) What you must confront
3) What you need to know
4) What you attain

OUTLOOK SPREAD

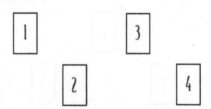

1) Outlook for the situation, event, or project
2) What/who will help
3) What this will lead to
4) How you will feel about the outcome

STRENGTH SPREAD

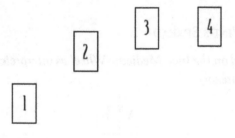

1) Your greatest strength
2) How you can enhance this strength
3) How you can apply it to a relationship, project, or event
4) What this strength brings you

TRAVEL SPREAD

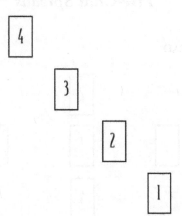

1) Surrounding influences of your upcoming trip
2) What you need to know about this trip, things that may be hidden
3) What you will learn or understand as a result of this trip
4) Outcome

WINDOW SPREAD

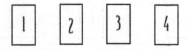

1) Current physical state
2) Current mental state
3) Current emotional state
4) Current spiritual state

Five-Card Spreads

BELIEF SPREAD

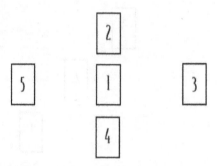

1) What you desire
2) The root belief that is blocking your attainment
3) Bridge belief that links 2 and 4
4) New belief coming into your life
5) Result/outcome of new belief

DIRECTION SPREAD

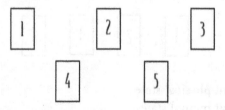

1) Your current life direction
2) The lesson you're learning
3) What you're moving toward
4) Your long-term objective
5) What will help you attain your objective

FOR OR AGAINST SPREAD

1) What you have
2) What you need to know about what's coming up
3) What you want
4) What works for or against you in the future
5) What you get

FRENCH SPREAD

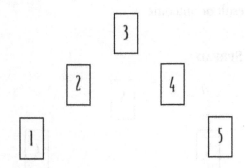

1) Things happening now
2) Hopes and dreams
3) Strength and security
4) Support or opposition
5) Something in the future that may surprise you

MAGIC STAR SPREAD

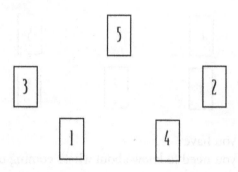

1) The nature of the problem, situation, or question
2) The cause of the problem, reason for asking, or point of interest
3) Factors to be considered
4) The solution, advice, or comment given
5) End result or outcome

MIRROR SPREAD

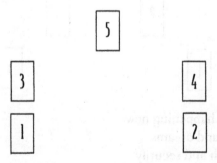

Quite often, the qualities we dislike in another person are qualities in ourselves that we aren't crazy about, either. In this way, the Mirror Spread addresses our shadow selves as well as our projections. The fifth position, what is really there, is actually a summation of a relationship's weaknesses or strengths.

1) The image: how you see the other person
2) The reflection: how the other person sees himself
3) What the other person represents to you
4) What you represent to the other person
5) What is really there

MONEY SPREAD

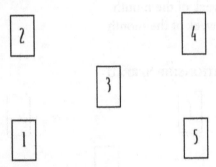

1) Financial foundation
2) Money coming into your life very soon
3) Money opportunities you may want to consider more closely
4) Who or what project will bring in new money
5) Result

MONTHLY SPREAD

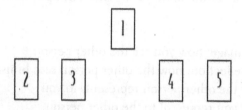

1) General atmosphere of the upcoming month
2) First week of the month
3) Second week of the month
4) Third week of the month
5) Fourth week of the month

NEW-RELATIONSHIP SPREAD

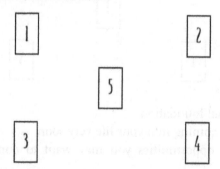

1) What you are bringing to the relationship
2) What the other person is bringing to the relationship
3) Will you be happy in this relationship?
4) Will the other person be happy in this relationship?
5) Will the relationship last?

WHEEL SPREAD

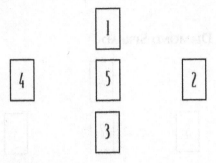

1) The present situation
2) Waning influences
3) Hidden or unconscious influences
4) Emerging influences
5) Synthesis: what will reconcile and unify the other four factors in the reading

YES/NO SPREAD

Shuffle a deck so that some of the cards are reversed cards and deal out five, seven, or nine cards. The middle card always counts as two points and the others as one point each. If the majority are upright, the answer is yes; vice versa means no. If the total points for yes and no are equal, then the cards are refusing to give a definite answer.

1–2) What happened in the past
3) What is happening now
4–5) What may happen in the future

Six-Card Spreads

BASEBALL DIAMOND SPREAD

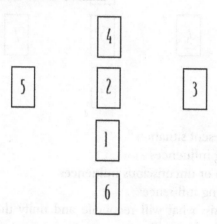

1) Home plate: Where you are now, a project or situation that is just beginning
2) Pitcher's mound: What is coming at you, an event or a person connected to something that is entering your life
3) First base: Step one. Where you are headed, the first phase of your new situation
4) Second base: Step two. Where you are headed, the next phase of your new situation
5) Third base: Step three. Where you are headed, the final phase of your new situation
6) Home plate: The result. The resolution or outcome of your new situation

EXPLORATION SPREAD

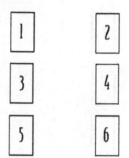

1) Situation now
2) Past belief that led to now
3) Lesson learned
4) How it helped you
5–6) New paths and how you'll feel about them

LADLE SPREAD

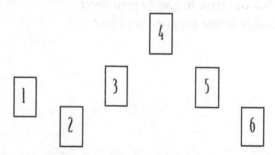

1) Root of question, the concern, the issue
2) What is hidden
3) What is emerging
4) What is visible now
5) What you scoop out
6) Resolution: how it affects you

LOVE SPREAD

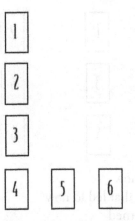

1) Your past experience in love
2) Your current experience in love
3) What you want from a love relationship
4) What you need from a love relationship
5) What you have to give to your lover
6) Possible future experience in love

LUCK SPREAD

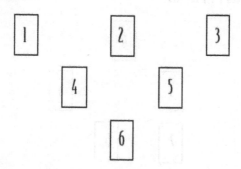

1) The overview for your luck factor
2) How this luck factor will affect your life
3) The area in which the luck may appear
4) Who or what will enter your life as a result of this luck
5) How this luck will help you attain what you desire
6) Timing—using aces only
       ace rods—spring
       ace cups—summer
       ace coins—autumn
       ace swords—winter

PROSPERITY SPREAD

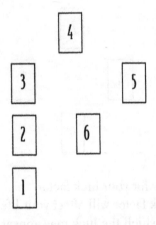

1) The area of your life where you prosper now
2) The area in which you would like to prosper in the future
3) What you need to do to cultivate that future prosperity
4) Who or what will help or hinder you
5) Something you need to be aware of
6) Your ultimate attainment

RAINBOW SPREAD

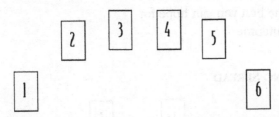

1) Rain: what is holding you back from attaining your heart's desire
2) Drizzle: first steps you can take toward achieving what you want
3) Clearing: who or what helps you
4) Sunshine: best you can hope for
5) Rainbow: short-term advice
6) Pot of gold: long-term outcome

SHORT CELTIC CROSS

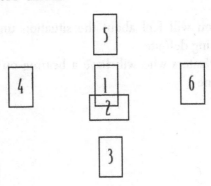

1) Past experience
2) Where you are now

3) Near future
4) Your future environment
5) The best you can hope for
6) Outcome

TIMING SPREAD

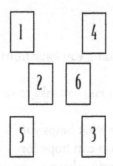

1) The root of the question
2) Where the situation is now
3) Where the situation will be within _____ (state time frame)
4) How you will feel about the situation until you know something definite
5) People/factors who will have a bearing on the situation
6) Outcome

Seven-Card Spreads

CHAKRA SPREAD

```
        ┌───┐
        │ 7 │
        └───┘

        ┌───┐
        │ 6 │
        └───┘

        ┌───┐
        │ 5 │
        └───┘

        ┌───┐
        │ 4 │
        └───┘

        ┌───┐
        │ 3 │
        └───┘

        ┌───┐
        │ 2 │
        └───┘

        ┌───┐
        │ 1 │
        └───┘
```

1) Root chakra. Color red, located at base of the spine. Self-preservation, grounding, energy level, vitality, and roots
2) Spleen chakra. Color orange, located near the genitals. Sexuality, emotions, survival of the species, nurturing
3) Solar plexus chakra. Color yellow, located in the solar plexus. Ego projection, how you use or express vital energies, digestive functions

4) Heart chakra. Color green, located in the center of the chest. Universal love, healing, compassion, understanding

5) Throat chakra. Color blue, located in the throat. Speech, self-expression, communication

6) Third-eye chakra. Color indigo, located in the center of the brow. Visions, fantasies, dreams, psychic ability, visualization of thoughts

7) Crown chakra. Color violet, located just above the top of the head. Our cosmic connection through which the Source manifests. Higher aspirations, desire for truth and knowledge

CHILD SPREAD

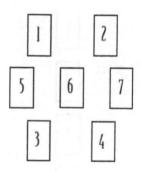

1) What the child came into this life to learn
2) Where she is now in her life
3) Where she shines
4) Something about this child you need to know
5) Where she is headed over the next _____ (state time frame)
6) Something that will impact this child's life over the next _____ (state time frame)
7) What she will achieve

CONSEQUENCES SPREAD

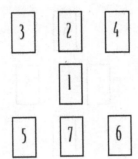

1) Your problem
2) Root of your problem
3) Past
4) Future
5) Advice
6) Outside influences
7) Final outcome

HARVEST SPREAD

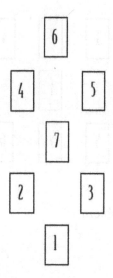

1) What you want
2) What seeds you need to sow to get what you want
3) What new belief you need in order to promote growth
4) Who or what helps you
5) What challenges you face
6) What you harvest
7) The key to the big picture

LOLLYPOP SPREAD

(Yesenia Garcia)

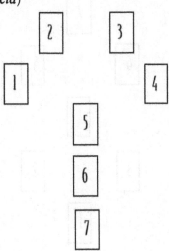

1) Home
2) School
3) Family
4) Friends
5) What you like to do now
6) What you would like to do in the future
7) What/who can help

MAGIC STAR SPREAD

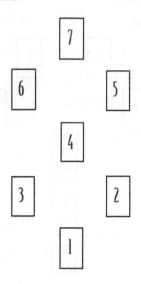

1) The past: root of the question
2) The present: your current position as related to the past
3) Immediate future: what may come to pass
4) Heart of the matter: your true feelings about the question asked
5) Unconscious influences: forces taking shape beneath the surface
6) Conscious desires: ideas, thoughts, feelings that are out in the open
7) Outcome: resolution

MANIFESTATION SPREAD

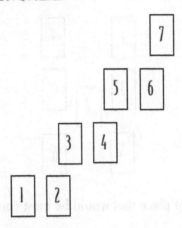

1–2) An area in your life you want to change
3–4) Your blessings now
5–6) How to use your blessings for transformation
  7) What you achieve through this merging

MOVE SPREAD

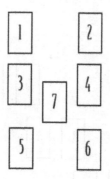

1) The kind of place that would be most conducive to your well-being
2) Your chances of moving within the next _____ (state time frame)
3) How you will find your special place
4) Something you need to know about this spot
5) What needs to happen before you can move
6) Something you need to consider about this place
7) Outcome

PET SPREAD

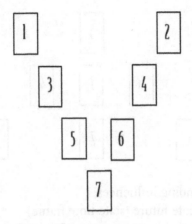

1) What your pet is trying to tell you
2) What your pet is feeling right now, what it desires
3) What you can do to help your pet
4) What your pet needs most at this time
5) Your pet's general health
6) Something your pet will need or feel in the near future
7) Overall outlook for your pet

PYRAMID SPREAD

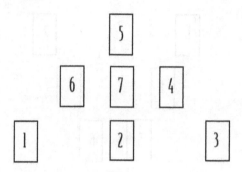

1–2) Surrounding influences
3–4) Immediate future (state time frame)
5–6) Long-term future (state time frame)
 7) Outcome

QUESTION AND ANSWER SPREAD

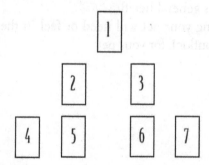

1) The question
2) Your reasons for asking
3) The root of the problem
4) Factors to be considered
5) Advice

6) One result of your current actions
7) A second possible result of your current actions

REALITY SHIFT SPREAD

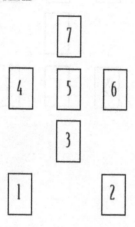

1) The directions you're giving your inner self now
2) How your external reality reflects this
3) How to empower your inner self to change your reality
4) How your outer self will respond to this new directive
5) How your life will shift as a result
6) What you will create
7) Your new path

WEEKLY SPREAD

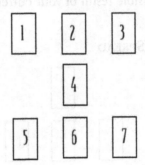

1) Day one
2) Day two
3) Day three
4) Day four
5) Day five
6) Day six
7) Day seven

Eight-Card Spreads

BIRD SPREAD

(Megan MacGregor)

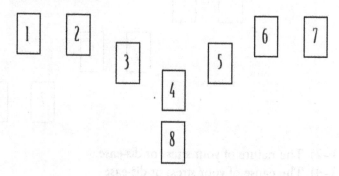

1–2) Where you are now
  3) How you get to where you want to be
  4) Where you're headed
  5) What you find along the way
6–7) What you learn
  8) How your journey ends

DIS-EASE SPREAD

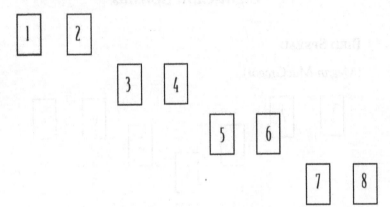

1-2) The nature of your stress or dis-ease
3-4) The cause of your stress or dis-ease
5-6) Who or what can help
7-8) The resolution or outcome

HEALTH AND HAPPINESS SPREAD

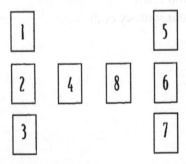

1) The state of your health in the past
2) Current state of your health
3) Possible future state of your health

4) What/who can help you to improve or maintain your health
5) What made you happy in the past
6) What makes you happy now
7) Possible event that will make you happy in the future
8) What/who helps augment your sense of happiness and well-being

HEART SPREAD

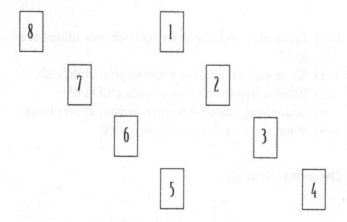

1) The primary issue that concerns you/your deepest desire
2) The most important factor involved in this issue (usually a past emotion)
3) How you can change this factor if it's blocking you or how you can enhance it if it's not blocking you
4) What will occur as a result of this action
5) What you may not see about this issue or desire in the near future
6) Challenges you may face in the near future
7) How this may affect you
8) What you ultimately attain concerning this issue or desire

ONLY-CHILD SPREAD

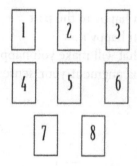

1–3) Personality and character traits of your minor or adult child
   4) Some past situation or event in your child's life
   5) What is happening now in your child's life
   6) Something that may happen in your child's future
7–8) What you can do to help your child

OVERVIEW SPREAD

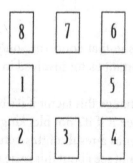

1) Home
2) Business
3) Relationships

4) Fame and achievements
5) Adversity
6) Acquisitions
7) Restrictions
8) Comprehensive overview

TRAITS SPREAD

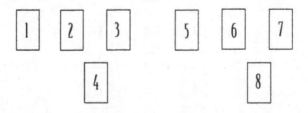

This spread was designed for two children but can easily be expanded to include more. Follow the format of the existing spread and add the additional placements.

1–3) Personality and character traits of your older child
   4) What you can do to help your older child
5–7) Personality and character traits of your younger child
   8) What you can do to help your younger child

Nine-Card Spreads

BIRTHDAY SPREAD

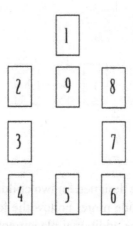

1) Where you are now
2) Where you would like to be on your next birthday
3) What empowers you
4) What you need to create to bring you closer to your goals
5) Your current material state
6) Your current emotional state
7) Your current spiritual state
8) What stands in opposition to your objectives
9) What you need to do this year to make your dreams come true

FUTURE SPREAD

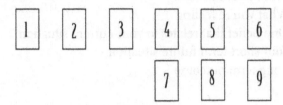

1-2) What happened in the past
3-4) What is happening now
5-6) What may happen in the near future
7-9) What may happen in the distant future

HORSESHOE SPREAD

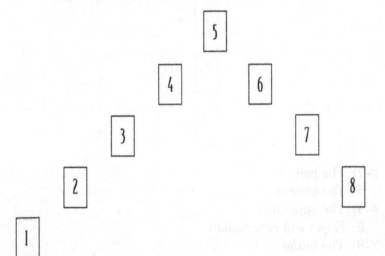

1) Your current situation
2) How other people affect you
3) How your surroundings affect you

4) How you respond to information from your inner self
5) What you're thinking
6) What you're feeling
7) One belief that relates to your current situation
8) Your short-term future situation
9) Long-term outcome

MAGIC CROSS

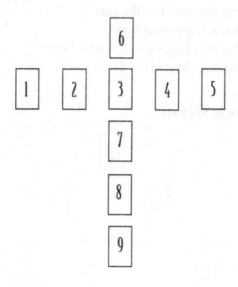

1–2) The past
  3) The present
4–5) The opposition
  6) Hopes and expectations
7–9) The future

RELATIONSHIP SPREAD

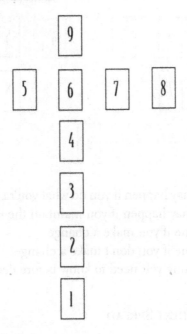

1) How you see the other person
2) How the other person sees you
3) What you need
4) What the other person needs
5) Where the relationship is now
6) Where you would like the relationship to go
7) Where the other person would like it to go
8) Factors to be considered
9) The end result

SHOULD YOU OR SHOULDN'T YOU SPREAD

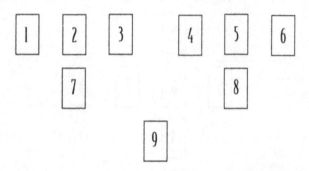

1–3) What may happen if you do what you're contemplating
4–6) What may happen if you maintain the status quo
   7) Outcome if you make a change
   8) Outcome if you don't make a change
   9) Something you need to know before deciding

TREASURE-CHEST SPREAD

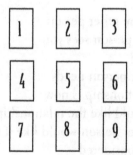

1) Diamonds: Where you shine. Major talents, abilities, and assets that you have
2) Pearls: What you know. Knowledge and information that you have incorporated into your life

3) Gold coins: What you have. Money and material possessions currently available to you
4) Emeralds: Who you know. Relationships that are now part
   of your life
5) Platinum chains: What's holding you back. Things or
   people in your life that you need to release
6) Sapphires: Where you could shine. Emerging talents, assets, and abilities
7) Quartz crystals: What you're learning. Knowledge and
   information that you could incorporate into your life
8) Rubies: Who you may soon know. Relationships that are
   entering your life
9) Unpolished diamonds: Your hidden lights. Assets and talents that you can develop

Who/What/Where Spread

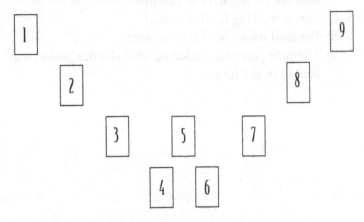

1) Where do you need to be going?
2-3) Who or what do you need to consider in getting there?
4-5) Who or what will help guide you?

6-7) What is coming up in the next four weeks that you need to know about?

8) How will it affect you?

9) What you ultimately achieve regarding this question

WRITERS' SPREAD

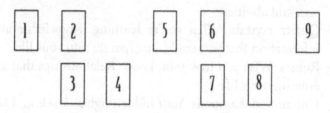

1-2) Past pertaining to this project

3-4) Something you need to know about this project that may not be apparent to you now

5-6) Forces working for this project

7-8) Personal meaning of this project

9) Ultimate outcome, including what else this project may lead to in the future

X-LOVER SPREAD

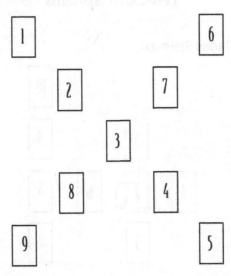

1) Past history of your relationship
2) Where you are now
3) Where your ex is now
4) What you really feel about getting back together
5) What your ex really feels about getting back together
6) Who or what opposes what you want
7) Who or what can help you get what you want
8) Something you may not know about the situation
9) Outcome or resolution

Ten-Card Spreads

CELTIC CROSS SPREAD

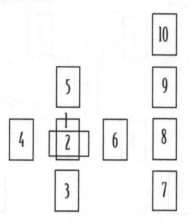

1) Cover. Surrounding influences, general atmosphere
2) Crossing. (Placed sideways across card 1.) Opposing forces, negative or positive
3) Foundation. Past basis of the matter
4) Behind you. Influences that are passing away
5) Crowning. Possible future event, forces taking shape
6) Before you. Forces already in motion that may manifest themselves in the future
7) Feelings. Fear, apprehension
8) Opinions. What others think about the matter
9) Hopes. Aspirations, goals, dreams, desires, fears
10) Outcome. The resolution or final outcome

LOST AND FOUND SPREAD

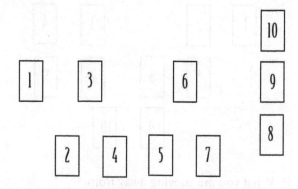

1) The object that is lost
2) Something you need to know about this loss
3–4) Where to begin your search
5) Who or what will help
6–7) Factors to be considered in your search
8–10) Outcome

Moving On Spread

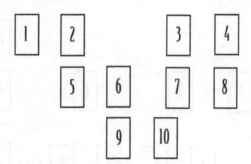

1–2) What you are moving away from
3–4) What you are moving toward
5–6) Things to consider before taking action
7–8) Reasons to move on
9–10) Outcome

ONGOING-RELATIONSHIP SPREAD

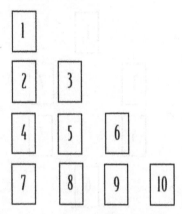

1) Past history of the relationship
2) Your past experience in the relationship
3) Your partner's past experience in the relationship
4) Your current experience in the relationship
5) Your partner's current experience in the relationship
6) The relationship in the present
7) What you may experience in the future in this relationship
8) What your partner may experience in the future in this relationship
9) Where the relationship is headed
10) Outcome: what may happen in this relationship in the future

TREE OF LIFE SPREAD

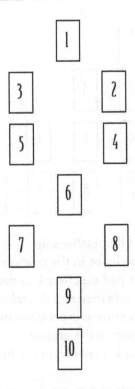

This spread ties the tarot to a complex system of philosophy and meditation derived from the ancient Jewish mystical teachings known as Kabbalah. As in the Chakra Spread, the cards are read from the bottom up.

When you have completed your reading, fan out the remaining cards and choose one to be the *Daat* card. This card goes midway between cards six and one. It represents the hidden knowledge that can help you achieve your highest aspirations.

It's possible to do an entire life reading with this spread, using all the cards in the deck. One card is selected as the significator, removed from the pack, and set to one side. Then seven cards are placed at each number on the tree and the remaining seven cards, which comprise the *Daat* pack, are set aside.

The *Daat* pack is used at the end of each phase to qualify and enlarge upon the reading. The cards are shuffled and spread out three times in this life reading: once for the past, a second time for the present, and a third time for the future. A complete Tree of Life reading takes several hours and tends to be comprehensive, so you probably won't do it more than once a year.

10) *Malkut* (kingdom): outcome, home, material world, physical body, daily life, the practical basis of the situation

9) *Yesod* (foundation): psychic centers, imagination, fantasy, habits, past lives, the subconscious foundations of the matter

8) *Hod* (splendor, glory): thoughts, knowledge of truth and untruth, verbal expression and communication, crafts, skills, science and technology

7) *Netzach* (victory, lastingness): love, eros, instincts, the arts, inspiration, feelings, beauty, pleasure

6) *Tiferet* (beauty): individuality, self, identity, health, tendency to sacrifice for others, intention, central goal or purpose

5) *Gievurah* (severity, strength): force, conquest, challenges, conflict, readjustment, obstacles, disharmonies, aggression, expressions of power, leadership

4) *Chesed* (mercy, grace): virtues, opportunities, gifts, resources, helpers, assistance, recognition, power

3) *Bina* (understanding): inner knowing and understanding, mother, anima, yin, coming to terms with limitations, ability to bring ideas into form

2) *Chochma* (wisdom): creative power, outer values and ideas, father, animus, yang, the potential for wisdom and knowledge, the essence

1) *Keter* (crown) highest ideals, sense of purpose and meaning, means of reconciliation, source or reason for your question

WEATHER SPREAD

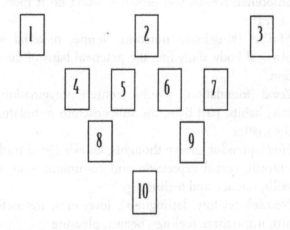

1–2) Thunderstorms: who or what troubles you
  3) Fog: what is hidden or unexpected
4–5) Snow: challenges
6–7) Partly cloudy: minor glitches
8–9) Beach day: where your life shines
 10) Resolution/culmination

WHAT'S GOING ON? SPREAD

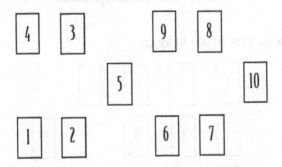

1-2) What's going on now, including what you may not see
3-4) Two upcoming events that influence the outcome
   5) Where the issue is headed
6-7) What you can expect based on the patterns of the present moment
8-9) How you can change it if you don't like it
  10) Overall outcome

Eleven-Card Spreads

FORK IN THE ROAD SPREAD

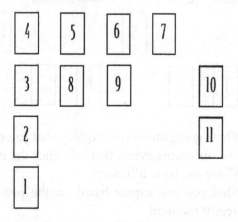

1-2) Current situation
3-4) What is hidden
5-7) Strongest possible outcome at this time based on present pattern/energy
8-9) Also a possible outcome
10-11) What *you* can do to experience the best possibility

JOB SPREAD

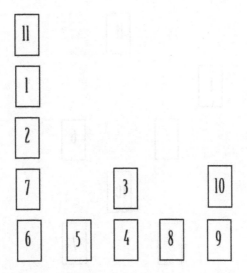

1) What you want for yourself
2) Who or what will help
3) What you should focus on
4) The turning point: the event that changes things
5) A possible new direction in employment/work
6) Synchronistic signal: an important event on this new path that you'll recognize when it happens
7) Ultimate attainment on this path
8) A second possible direction
9) Synchronistic signal: an important event on this path that you will recognize when it happens
10) Ultimate achievement on this path
11) What you need to know to choose the direction that suits you

Room Spread

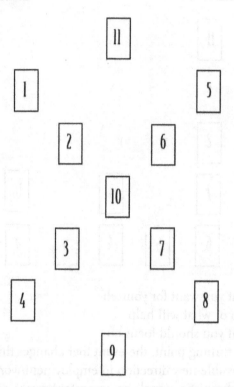

1) Living room: friends, social contacts, group activities
2) Family room: immediate family—parents, siblings, spouse, kids, pets
3) Kitchen: health, physical self
4) Den: work, finances
5) Utility room: what you need to tend to, take care of
6) Cellar: what is hidden or what has accumulated in your life that you may not be aware of
7) Garage: what is parked in your life that needs attention
8) Bedroom: a belief that connects 9 and 10

9) Rear door: what/who is leaving your life
10) Front door: what/who is arriving in your life
11) Loft: what you ultimately achieve

TURNING-POINT SPREAD

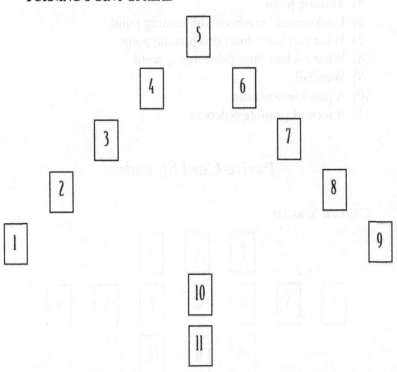

Pay special attention to the card in position five; it may be triggered by an event, a particular person, or a sudden change in a core belief. If the nine of cups appears in positions nine or ten, it takes precedence over any of the darker cards that may show up.

1) Surrounding circumstances
2) Something you need to know about the present circumstances
3) Belief patterns that have led to this point
4) Bridge event that leads to the turning point
5) Turning point
6) Unexpected benefits of the turning point
7) What you learn from this turning point
8) What evolves from this turning point
9) Windfall
10) A possible outcome
11) A second possible outcome

Twelve-Card Spreads

CAREER SPREAD

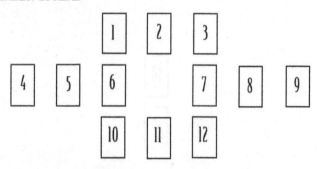

1–3) Current situation regarding your job or unemployment
4–6) Past influences that helped bring about the current situation
7–9) What helps change the current situation
10–12) What the future brings

DREAM INTERPRETATION SPREAD

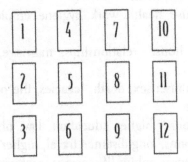

1–3) Images that describe your dream
4–6) What the dream images mean
7–9) How they affect your waking life
10–12) How you can best use this information

HOROSCOPE SPREAD

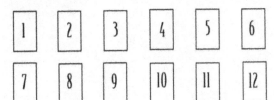

1) First house: All beginnings. Personality, potential, outward appearance
2) Second house: what one values, tangible assets, material possessions
3) Third house: mental activity, communication, writing, siblings, neighbors
4) Fourth house: private life, home, family, and parents

5) Fifth house: creativity, emotions, romance, children, art, and entertainment
6) Sixth house: health, work, hygiene, employees, and service
7) Seventh house: relationships, marriage, partnerships, contracts
8) Eighth house: sex, death, legacies, the occult, external influence
9) Ninth house: higher education, law, philosophy, religion, dreams, long-distance travel, higher mind
10) Tenth house: public life, career, profession, ambitions, honors
11) Eleventh house: friends, associations, groups, hopes, wishes
12) Twelfth house: unconscious mind, karma, secrets, hidden limitations

SHE, HE, IT SPREAD

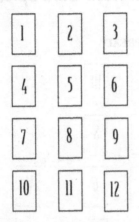

1) What you want
2) What the other person wants
3) What the relationship wants
4) What you "really" want
5) What the other person "really" wants
6) What the relationship "really" wants
7) What you need
8) What the other person needs
9) What the relationship needs
10) What you get
11) What the other person gets
12) What the relationship gets

Thirteen-Card Spreads

EXPECTATION SPREAD

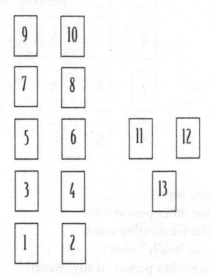

1–2) Your expectations in the past about _____
3–4) Your expectations now about _____
5–6) Your expectations in the future about _____
7–8) How those expectations may manifest themselves
9–10) How the manifestation may change your life
11–12) Ultimate outcome/achievement
13) A new path that will develop from this outcome

KIDS' SPREAD

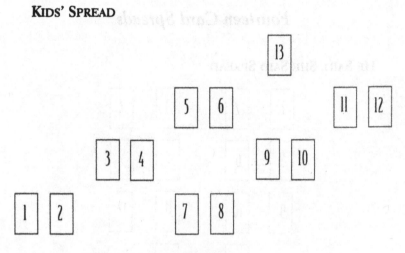

1-2) What you think you want
3-4) What you know you want
5-6) What you feel about what you want
7-8) What you fear the most
9-10) What makes you happiest
11-12) The best way to attain what you want
   13) What you will attain/achieve over the next _____
      (time frame)

Fourteen-Card Spreads

HE SAID, SHE SAID SPREAD

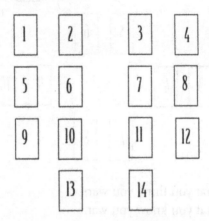

1–2) What he likes about the relationship
3–4) What she likes about the relationship
5–6) What he doesn't like about the relationship
7–8) What she doesn't like about the relationship
9–10) What he would like to see happen in the relationship
11–12) What she would like to see happen in the relation-
　　　ship
13–14) Outcome: where the relationship is headed

PAST-LIFE SPREAD

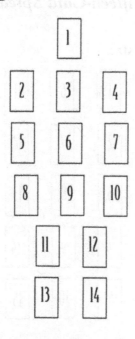

1) Basic soul nature coming into this past life
2) Environment
3) Early years
4) Education
5) Accomplishments
6) Occupation
7) Social status
8) Relationships
9) Family life
10) Death
11–12) Lessons learned during this past life
13–14) How this past life affects your current life

Fifteen-Card Spreads

PLANETARY SPREAD

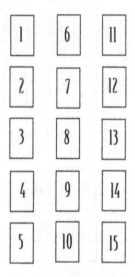

1) Sun: vitality, will, male principle
2) Moon: receptivity, feelings, female principle
3) Mercury: mentality, communications, dexterity
4) Venus: love, peace, beauty, harmony
5) Mars: sex, war, energy, courage
6) Jupiter: success, luck, expansion, growth
7) Saturn: responsibility, duty, limitations, security
8) Uranus: originality, freedom, independence, genius
9) Neptune: idealism, illusion, spirituality, mystery
10) Pluto: regeneration, transformation, power, research
11) North Node: associations, unions, connections
12) South Node: past life connections
13) Ascendant: personal inclinations

14) Mid-Heaven: Career, status, or calling
15) Vertex: Fated role

SNAPSHOT SPREAD

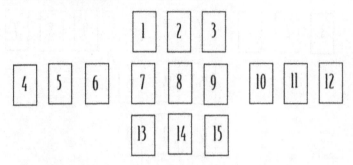

1-3) Career
4-6) Home
7-9) Finances
10-12) Relationships
13-15) Future

WISH SPREAD

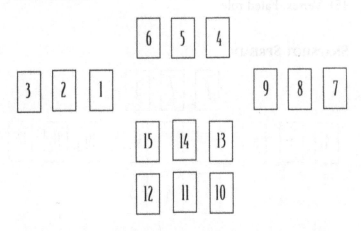

If the wish card, the nine of cups, appears in any spot except positions seven, eight, and nine, the wish, at least in part, will come true. The closer the wish card falls to the first card, the sooner it will be realized.

1–3) What surrounds you
4–6) The factors that describe your wish
7–9) The factors that oppose your wish
10–12) What will come into your home
13–15) What you will realize

Sixteen-Card Spreads

BOHEMIAN SPREAD

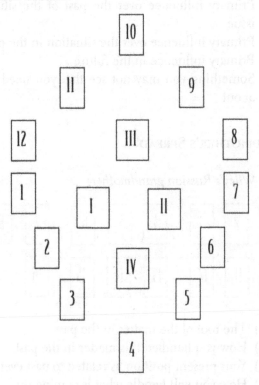

The outer circle of numbers should be laid out with minor arcana cards only. Then, using just the major arcana cards, draw four and place them in the inner circle in the I, II, III, IV positions.

 1) The root of the question, the primary issue
2–3) The past
4–6) The present situations
7–12) The future
   I) Primary influence over the past of the situation or issue
  II) Primary influence over the situation in the present
 III) Primary influence in the future
  IV) Something you may not see that you need to know about

GRANDMOTHER'S SPREAD

(Renie Wiley's Russian grandmother)

1–3) The root of the matter in the past
4–6) How you handled this matter in the past
7–9) Your present position as related to past events
10–12) How you will handle what is coming up
13–15) Probable future events, forces taking shape
  16) The culmination and resolution of the question

Seventeen-Card Spread

HORIZON SPREAD

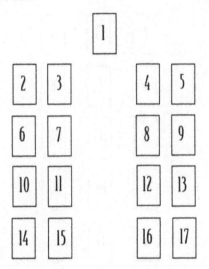

1) Key card
2-5) What's above the horizon
6-9) What's at the horizon
10-13) What's beneath the horizon
14-17) What's next to rise

Eighteen-Card Spread

VISUALIZATION SPREAD

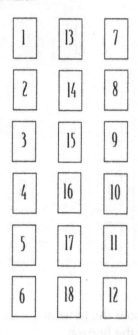

The first column represents the present. The third column is about six weeks from now, the second column is three months from now. If you draw cards in any of the columns that you don't like, then substitute a card that expresses what you desire for yourself in that particular area.

Post your ideal cards or copies of them where you can see them often. Spend a few minutes each day focusing on these cards and imagining their reality in as much detail and with as much emotion as possible.

1,13,7) Home/family
2,14,8) Romance
3,15,9) Career/work
4,16,10) Money
5,17,11) Spiritual
6,18,12) Overall

Nineteen-Card Spread

BRIDGE SPREAD

1	4	7	10	13	16	
2	5	8	11	14	17	19
3	6	9	12	15	18	

1–3) Past
4–6) Bridge to the present: events, beliefs, what you might not be aware of
7–9) Now
10–12) Bridge to the future: events, beliefs, what you might not be aware of
13–15) Near future
16–18) Bridge to outcome: things both hidden and visible that work for/against you
19) Ultimate outcome

Twenty-Card Spread

NEW YEAR'S SPREAD

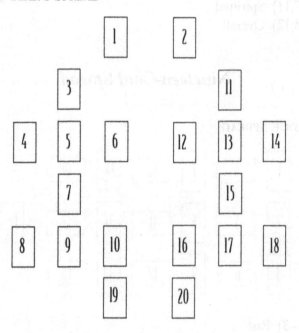

1–2) What you're bringing forward from the prior year
  3) Winter overview
  4) January outlook
  5) February outlook
  6) March outlook
  7) Spring overview
  8) April outlook
  9) May outlook
 10) June outlook
 11) Summer overview

12) July outlook
13) August outlook
14) September outlook
15) Autumn overview
16) October outlook
17) November outlook
18) December outlook
19–20) What you will carry forward into next year

Twenty-one-Card Spread

ANYTHING GOES SPREAD

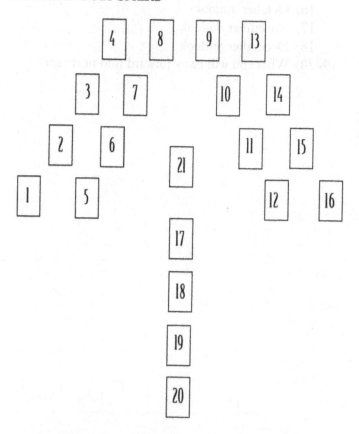

1–4) The issue/situation now

5–8) What you really desire

9–12) How your core beliefs mesh/conflict with that desire

13–16) What you should do to alter your reality, the steps you
should take

17–20) The content of your manifestation, how it appears in
your life
21) What comes after that

Twenty-two-Card Spread

POINT-OF-POWER SPREAD

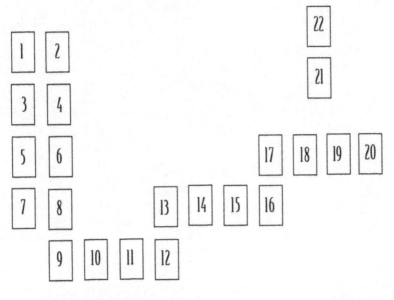

1–2) Your situation now
3–4) What you want most to change
5–6) What/who will help
7–8) Beliefs to cultivate in order to attain what you desire
9–10) Events that spring from these new beliefs
11–12) What you'll feel about these events
13–14) A second branch of events that may emerge

15–16) What you'll feel about these events
17–18) A third branch of events that may emerge
19–20) How you'll feel about these events
   21) The power you must cultivate in the present to create the future you want
   22) Your ultimate achievement

Twenty-three-Card Spread

BUSTING LOOSE SPREAD

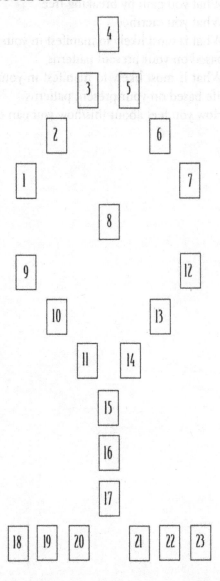

1–3) What you want to break away from

4–7) Why you want to break away

8) What links you most strongly to the future you're trying to create

9–11) What you gain by breaking free

12–14) What you sacrifice

15–17) What is most likely to manifest in your personal life, based on your present patterns

18–20) What is most likely to manifest in your professional life based on your present patterns

21–23) How you feel about this/how you can change it

Twenty-four-Card Spread

DOUBLE HOROSCOPE SPREAD

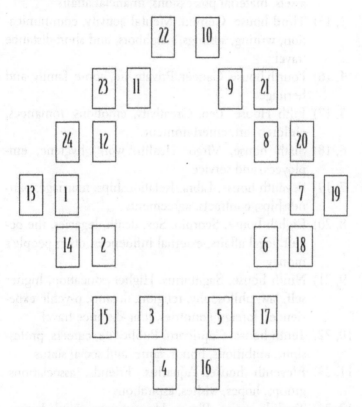

Separate the major arcana cards from the rest of the deck. Shuffle and deal a dozen cards around the wheel from positions 1 through 12. Return the remaining majors to the deck, shuffle again and deal a dozen more cards around the wheel from positions 13 to 24.

1, 13) First house, Aries. Beginnings, personality, potential, outward appearance, constitution, interests, and attitudes

2, 14) Second house, Taurus. What one values, tangible assets, material possessions, financial affairs

3, 15) Third house, Gemini. Mental activity, communication, writing, siblings, neighbors, and short-distance travel

4, 16) Fourth house, Cancer. Private life, home, family, and heritage

5, 17) Fifth House, Leo. Creativity, emotions, romances, children, art, entertainment

6, 18) Sixth house, Virgo. Health, work, hygiene, employees, and service

7, 19) Seventh house, Libra. Relationships, marriage, partnerships, contracts, agreements

8, 20) Eighth house, Scorpio. Sex, death, legacies, the occult, legal affairs, external influences, other people's money

9, 21) Ninth house, Sagittarius. Higher education, higher self, law, philosophy, religion, dreams, psychic experiences, foreign countries, long-distance travel

10, 22) Tenth house, Capricorn. Public life, careers, professions, ambitions, honor, fame, and social status

11, 23) Eleventh house, Aquarius. Friends, associations, groups, hopes, wishes, aspirations

12, 24) Twelfth house, Pisces. Unconscious mind, karma, secrets, hidden limitations, self-undoing

7

Fitting It Together

Don't Panic

You're reading for someone outside of your immediate circle of friends and family, the cards are on the table, and you draw a complete blank. Panic flutters in your chest, adrenaline rushes through you, doors slam shut in your head. What do you do?

Take a deep breath and focus on the first two cards. Let the artwork speak to you. Allow your intuition to step in. Let's say the first two cards are the ace of swords and the three of cups and the woman has asked about a relationship she's involved in.

What does the ace tell you about her? Does the art on the card suggest sexuality? Aggression? Initiative? Say whatever

comes to mind. Now go through the same process with the
three of cups, then put the two together. Does the combination change the meaning? If so, how?

These two cards suggest that the relationship is a double-
edged sword, intensely sexual, and that she and the man enjoy
each other's company. There's a possibility it may end in
marriage. But if you add the Tower to the combination and
use the Past/Present/Future Spread for the three cards, the
picture changes somewhat.

The ace then becomes the card for the past position, indicating that the relationship was intensely sexual and that the
woman was most likely the aggressor. In the present, the three
of cups suggests celebration, happiness, and a possible marriage. But in the future, the Tower means that something
unexpected may slam into the relationship and completely
reverse things. The relationship, in fact, may fall apart.

Instead of ending the spread on this very dark note, the
individual would draw another card to find out what this
event is. Let's suppose she draws the queen of wands. Since
this is her significator, we now know she is the one who will be
affected by this unexpected event. But what about the event
itself? What is it? What will it entail? She draws yet another
card and pulls the six of swords.

Now the picture becomes clearer. The possible event depicted in the Tower is a move some distance from where she
lives now, possibly a move overseas. This will certainly affect
the relationship, but whether it's positive or negative will
depend entirely on the people involved, on their *free will*.
This is why it's vital that you never end a reading, even for
yourself, on a negative note.

Combinations

The easiest way to learn how to read combinations of cards is through practice. But there are several guidelines to remember:

- Look for the thread of the story.
- If a card doesn't make sense, pull another card or several more for clarification. If the cards still don't make sense, continue to the end of the reading, then do a second spread on the same question.
- If there's a predominance of majors in a particular combination, interpret them first in terms of large issues. Then look to the minors for hints on how these issues may manifest themselves in daily life.
- If court cards dominate a particular spread, describe the kind of person they represent and ask the person you're reading for if she recognizes the individual. If she doesn't, then read these as people who are about to enter her life or as types of energy that she will be dealing with in the near future.
- In the course of a reading, if new definitions about the cards or particular combinations come to mind, by all means use them. Later, jot them in your journal.

An example of this happened on the 900-line, with a young male caller who wanted to know how things looked generally for the next three months. We used the Ladle Spread and in the fourth and fifth positions—what is visible and what you scoop out—drew the four of swords and Judgement. We didn't know his situation, but interpreted the pair of cards accurately: he was currently in prison (four of swords) and was coming up for a parole hearing (Judgement) within three months.

Your Tarot Philosophy

By the time you start reading for other people, you'll have some sort of philosophy or theory about tarot and other divination systems, if you don't already. It will help you answer the most frequently asked questions:

- Does this stuff *really* work?
- *How* does it work?
- Will everything you say happen?
- Is the future depicted in the cards inevitable?
- Can I change what the cards say?

The only way you or the individuals you read for will be able to answer these questions is by keeping notes on the readings. If you're reading for yourself, simply use your journal. Jot down the date, time, question, general atmosphere of where you're reading, and the cards you draw. Check back through your journal periodically to see how you did.

Of course, some readings will be more accurate than others. This may be due to any number of variables. Over time, you will perceive a pattern to the accuracy that points to certain times and conditions being more conducive than others. So keep careful notes. When you're reading for other people, use a tape recorder. This allows them to refer to the readings periodically in order to gauge their accuracy.

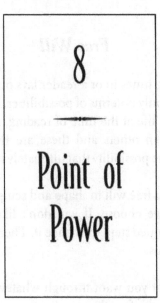

8

Point of Power

Each of us has a concept of what power is. We may not be able to define it specifically, but we know when we *don't* have it.

The dictionary defines power as "the ability to do, the capacity to act; a specific ability or faculty; a person or thing having great influence, force, or authority." The problem with this definition is that it doesn't mention that power, yours or anyone else's, stems from *this moment*, this second, this instant of your life, this *now*.

The present is what you're living. The present is your launchpad.

Free Will

When a psychic tunes in or a reader lays out cards, he or she sees the future only in terms of possibilities. Because of where you are in your life at the time of reading, some possibilities are stronger than others and these are the most likely to manifest. But the possibility that ultimately manifests depends entirely on *you*.

We all possess free will to shape and sculpt our destinies in whatever way we choose. If you don't like a reading, take positive, determined steps to change it. There are any number of ways to do this.

- Visualize what you want through whatever method works best for you and infuse the visualization with as much fervor and imagination as you can muster.
- Pick out the cards that represent the kind of reading you would like, have them blown up into posters, and hang them in your work area. They will serve as visual illustrations of what you hope to achieve.
- Take whatever steps are necessary to realign your life so that it's more in keeping with what you hope to achieve. If you're an elementary school teacher, for example, then it's more realistic to imagine yourself with your own business than as the CEO of IBM.
- Identify the core beliefs that are holding you back and work to change them. Begin by making small gestures that show your belief in your ability to achieve what you most desire. If you're looking for the perfect mate and have listed the qualities you want in such a person, then strive to bring your own life into line with those qualities as well.
- Perfect the art of manifestation by starting with small goals.

We have a friend who never fails to create a parking space in even the most crowded parking lots. Once you're able to do this on a regular basis, your confidence is bolstered and you can move on to larger goals: a raise, a new job, the ideal mate.

Personal empowerment begins now, this second. But if you're unsure of where or how to begin, work with the five-card Belief Spread and the Direction Spread.

One of the best examples of the power of visualization and manifestation happened to Rob, a windsurfer. He had gone windsurfing one afternoon on a lake near where he lived and had lost his wallet. He wasn't sure if he'd lost it on the way to the lake or while he was windsurfing, but the location was less important than the loss itself.

He didn't do any of the things people usually do when they lose their wallets. He didn't call any credit card companies, and he didn't apply for a new license. Instead, he waited, certain that he was going to find it.

For several days, he visualized the wallet in his possession and infused the image with vivid details: how it felt in his hands, the cool texture of the leather, the contents. Nothing happened, but he remained firm in his conviction.

That same week, a lawn-care man dropped by Rob's house, soliciting business. Rob already had someone to mow the lawn, but he and the man chatted, then the man left. Two days later, this same man was fishing in a lake near Rob's house and hooked a wallet. He recognized Rob's photo on his driver's license and returned it to him.

The odds against this are probably astronomical, particularly when you consider that the guy who hooked the wallet had been by the house only a few days before. But it illustrates how belief, intent, a focused will, and imagination are the most important elements in creating the kind of reality you want. Cards, psychics, runes, the *I Ching*, whatever vehicle you use, will reflect that reality as it exists, as it changes, as it solidifies.

Beliefs

"The tarot is the devil's work."
"Those cards can't tell you anything. It's just superstition."
"The what?"
"The tarot is evil."
"You really believe that stuff?"
"That's just Gypsy fortune-telling."

These statements are all indicative of various belief systems you will undoubtedly encounter at some point in your work with the tarot. Maybe your husband or wife is skeptical of divination systems in general. Perhaps your sister's religion lumps tarot with the devil. Maybe your friends have never even heard of the tarot.

The impact of other people's belief systems on you will depend on how deeply you work with the cards and whether you integrate what you learn into who you are. If you're confronted with negativity and skepticism from the people you're closest to, then it might behoove you to identify what you really believe about your work with the tarot.

Is there, perhaps, some part of you that clings to a religious tenet handed down somewhere in your childhood that says divination is wrong or sinful? If so, does that belief still serve a purpose in your life? Are you involved with someone who dismisses your work with the tarot as a passing whim or as superstitious nonsense? If so, why are you involved with that person? What does this relationship satisfy in your life? Is it perhaps a habit you've outgrown?

These are the kinds of questions that may confront you. And ultimately, the answers you find will empower you because they allow you a deeper understanding of who you are.

The cards, like any divination tool, are simply a means to knowledge. Runes, the *I Ching*, palmistry, or soggy leaves at the bottom of a teacup may work as well or better for you. At some point, the tool you use may become incidental to the process of reading for yourself or someone else; intuition takes over.

When this happens, it's as if some inner channel opens and you begin to pick up names. Detailed pictures form in your head. Or as one psychic put it, "The movie starts to roll." So let it roll. Trust whatever images you get, follow whatever impulses you feel into an undiscovered country.

The tarot is merely one tool among many that allows us to travel through the labyrinth of what makes us human. We hope that your journey surpasses our own.

The authors can be contacted at:
mac111@ix.netcom.com
phyllisvega@delphi.com

Index